SEEING BEYOND

SEEING BEYOND

Written by
Kelly Taylor Nutt

PUBLISHING
Christian Literature & Artwork
A BOLD TRUTH Publication

Dedication

Dedicated to:
My Mom and Dad: Robert and Shirley Taylor
My children: Robby, Ryan, Rusty, Rachal, and her husband
Billy, and all future spouses of my sons
My grandchildren: Robby, Erin, Haley, Jaydin, Ryan, Isaac,
Jacob, Ethan, Andrew, and any future descendants who may
be born, married or adopted into our family lineage.
My sister: Toni, and her husband Phillip
My nephew: Alex
My husband: William
My Saviour:

Jesus

Seeing Beyond
Copyright © 2016 Kelly Taylor Nutt
ISBN 13: 978-0-9981531-2-4

BOLD TRUTH PUBLISHING
Christian Literature & Artwork
300 West 41st ▪ Sand Springs, Oklahoma 74067
www.BoldTruthPublishing.com
beirep@yahoo.com

Printed in the USA.

Contents
■ *(sequential order)*

Contents
(sequential order)

Contents
(sequential order)

Contents
(sequential order)

Contents
(sequential order)

Contents
(sequential order)

Contents
(sequential order)

Contents
● (alphabetical order)

Contents
(alphabetical order)

Contents
(alphabetical order)

Contents
(alphabetical order)

Contents
(alphabetical order)

Contents
(alphabetical order)

Contents
(alphabetical order)

Foreword

Seeing Beyond

Before we knew Jesus
It was hard to see
Beyond ourselves

But once we see Him
It is hard to see anything else

He saw beyond the pain and guilt that attempts to cling to our hearts like a magnet. And He knows how to release us from the force that draws us back to it.

He saw beyond our tortured souls and reached that place of our greatest need.

He saw beyond the fences we have carefully constructed around our hearts to guard it.

He saw beyond our angry countenance and reached directly into our hearts.

He saw beyond us as we excused ourselves from service because we thought we had nothing to offer the King.

He saw beyond who we are now and sees who we will become.

He refused to see beyond what His Father was doing and

lived only to please and glorify His Father.

He saw beyond the nails, the crown of thorns, the humiliation and ridicule He would endure at the cross.

He saw beyond that day of obedience and sacrifice and saw the sea of humanity desperately in need of a Deliverer. His eyes were fixed on each individual with their hands reaching up toward the sky as they cried out, "Save us!"

Without hesitation, He submitted to the Father's will as His love and compassion for those who were in imminent danger were before His eyes.

He saw beyond.....

And loved who He saw.

Introduction

Within the pages of this book, is a collection of thoughts, poetry and short stories. Most of the poems are songs that I have rewritten as a poem.

A lot of them are evangelistic in nature. Many are written symbolically and include biblical principles and applied to life situations. Most of the stories are fictional, but a few are things He has taught me and I wrote into a story. Some are allegorical in nature. I suppose the writings are a mixture and written to people in all walks of life. To those who have never met Jesus, they are an introduction and an invitation. To those who have met Him, they are a reminder of the time when you first gave your heart to Him. To those who may have fallen away from Him, they are written to restore that relationship with the One you fell in love with. A returning to our first love. A re-kindling of the fire that once burned within us.

I have noticed that my writing style has changed as I have matured spiritually, and in my natural aging process.

A few of the poems are written with honesty about my current feelings at that time, and some are written during a time when I strayed away on the wrong path. Thankfully, He is in the process of restoring me to the place He was leading me to begin with.

Almost all of the writings are written to lead us to the One I love, the One I serve, the One and only true God......Jesus. *John 14:6 - Jesus answered, "I am the way and the truth and the life. No one comes to the Father except through me."*

I do acknowledge that the writings are beyond my abilities and I thank the Lord for helping me write them. I could not have done it without Him.

On the cover of the book is a photo of me when I was around four years old.

During my rebellious teenage years, my Mom laid that picture on my bed. The one she put there was one they had painted. The one on the cover is the black and white photograph. Out of anger, I ripped a little area on all four sides of the picture. The photo still has the rips in it, much to my dismay.

It is a reminder of how the enemy was trying to destroy me during that time, and throughout my adult years. Just as he attempts to destroy all of us by ripping our hearts and sifting us like wheat. The key word in the last sentence is "attempts." Thankfully, I did not rip the picture in half. Thankfully, the Lord did not allow the enemy to be successful in his attempts.

Hopefully some of the stories will minister to you as the Lord patches up the pieces of your fractured and splintered heart.

We all struggle with different areas of wounding. Some more than others. But we also have one thing in common. A Saviour Who was sent to heal the broken-hearted.

It is in honor of Him that I wrote this book.

Unto the Lamb,

Kelly Taylor Nutt

The Sound of Love

The sound of my breath
Is heard on the earth
Life-giving breath
Of My Spirit
Life to the nations

His breath is flowing with
A rhythmic sound
Constant
Never ceasing
Always giving life

Can you hear it?

Inhale His love
As He exhales
And releases life to His people
Like the wind
His breath is swirling in the air
Breathe deeply as life
Refreshes and fills
Your heart, your soul, your spirit

The sound of My love
Is heard on the earth
My heart beating

Crying out
Love to the nations

His heart is beating with
A rhythmic sound
Like the steady beat of a drum
It never stops its eternal beat

Can you hear the sound?

Rhythmic
Constant
Never-ceasing
Unchanging
Steady, steady, steady
His love poured out
With every beat of His heart
His never-ending love song
Beating out the rhythm of love
Crying out for Your people

His heart beat, His breath
Beating a rhythm of love
A rhythm of life

For you

Kelly Taylor Nutt, Copyright © 2016

Who is Like...

Who is like a mountain?
Who is like a river?
Who is like a fountain flowing down?
Come to the mountain
God's holy mountain
His voice will shake the hardened ground

Who is like our God?
Our holy God
Whose fire will burn sin away
Jump into this river
His cleansing water
Wash your sins away

Who is like the thunder?
Who is like the ocean?
Who is like the lightning?
When it hits the ground
Powerful, majestic, full of strength...He is

Who is like a whisper?
Whose touch is gentle?
Who speaks to us with a still, small voice
Tender, merciful, forgiving, full of compassion...He is

Where Jesus walks, power follows

The ground shakes.
Rumblings in the atmosphere are heard
as He cries out for His long, lost love..
And as the enemy runs from the ferociousness of the Lion.

Where Jesus walks, love follows.
Hearts are quieted as we understand
His deep love and compassion.

Shhh!

Listen to the sound of people running
and falling at His feet.

Jesus, the Lion...Jesus, the Lamb...
Everything is found in You!

When God...

When God speaks, life happens

Where Jesus walks, love happens

When He breathes, air is freshened

When He touches, healing flows

When His name is spoken, everyone hears it

When His blood was spilled, salvation came

When we cry for mercy, we attain it

When He preaches, hearts are changed

When we go to war, He goes before us

When we confess our sins, He forgives us

When we are weary, He sends rest

When we are thirsty, He releases water

When we are hungry, He fills us

When you need Him, He is there.

When you are lost, He will find you

When You shout for Your bride.....

We will go home

The Blood - The Out-pouring

The rhythm of His heart
As He was dying for humanity
Beat in a steady rhythm
Until it ceased

When His heartbeat pounded
For the last time
When the last breath in His lungs was released
From His mouth

It was finished!

His destiny was complete
He fulfilled His purpose
He was victorious!
In that glorious moment in time
At that split-second, salvation became available to us
It was ours to receive

During the hours He hung on the cross
I wonder how intense the battle was inside of His mind.
We only understand, to a degree, what happened to His body.

His heart was bleeding
His heart was beating
Pouring out love

For His Father and for His children

He was bruised for our iniquities.
He was despised and rejected of men.

The pain of rejection from His children
Probably added to His inner pain He experienced there.

But when His Father turned His face from His Son......
His heart probably broke into.

His heart poured out
His blood poured out
And splashed on the soil of the earth.
Every drop of blood that fell
On the streets of Jerusalem became
The path to life.
The trail of blood was actually a trail
Of love that continues to lead us to the cross,
Where He purchased us with His blood.

The sound of the blood
Falling and hitting the ground
Was a sound the enemy longed to hear.
He thought they could clean the streets
Of His blood, and erase and cover up the murder
Of an innocent man.

But the effects of His death and resurrection
Can never be erased or forgotten about.
Because His blood continues to cleanse.

It has not lessened in power.

The enemy thought he was the victor. He thought it would be over when Jesus took His last breath.

It was not.

The enemy will never be a victor.

He probably cringed when he heard Jesus victoriously speak His last words, *"It is finished."*

But he shook it off, because he was gloating as he saw the trail of blood. Admiring his accomplishments, he probably held his head high as all he had hoped for, seemingly, was complete.

I can imagine he pridefully proclaimed, "I have become like the Most High! I have killed His son!" He probably imagined himself sitting on the throne.

What he thought was his victory Was, in actuality, his eternal defeat.

Because three days later, Jesus' heart began to beat again. His lungs were again filled with the breath of God.

In an instant, He arose!

Kelly Taylor Nutt, Copyright © 2016

Hosanna!

When You rode the donkey into Jerusalem
Proclaiming silently Who You are…
You waited to see if the truth
That You were their long-awaited Messiah
Would be shown to them

As praise filled their hearts
So strong was the worship within them
They could not stop the praise that was rising
They could not keep silent!

And just as they were then,
We, Your people, can not keep the truth
Shut up in our hearts

We shout Hosanna!
You are the Messiah!
We declare today
That we know that You are
Who You said You are

We throw down our cloaks
We lay palm branches down
On the path where You will walk
Even on the road, the highways
Palm branches pave the way

Hosanna!

We bow
We turn
We turn to You

We honor and reverence the Messiah

The King of Glory is in our midst!

Pouring out Love

Every day I live, I want to pour into Jesus' hands…
My love

Because my sins caused the nails to be driven into them

I want to spend eternity pouring into His feet...
My adoration

Because I had a part in nailing them to the cross

Forever I will bow in honor and respect

As He wears
The robe He deserved
The crown He deserved
And receives the love He deserved

I want to pour into His wounds every ounce of love that I
have to give

Because He completely poured Himself out…
For us

The Rose Arose

The Rose, the Rose…Rose to bloom
The Rose, the Rose…Crushed and bruised
The Rose, the Rose…His fragrance loosed
The Rose, the Rose...The Rose of Sharon reigns!
The Rose, the Rose…Rose again!

At first the Rose was a bud. Every day of His life, the petals unfolded. One by one they opened up to reveal His beauty. Each petal represented a different aspect of His life. Until one day, each petal was completely opened.

The beauty of the Rose was breath-taking. People stared in awe as the Rose's true beauty was revealed.

But the time came for the Rose to die. His petals began to wilt. Soon, the Rose fell to the ground. People began to gather the petals to save, because they knew the fragrance was the greatest after it dies.

Three days later, those who had saved the petals were per-plexed. The petals were gone! A strong aroma filled the air. They began to follow the perfume.

The closer they got to the garden where the Rose had been planted, the stronger the fragrance was.

When they reached the garden, they could not believe what they saw. The dead Rose had come back to life! Never before had this happened. They rejoiced because they knew it had been replaced in their garden by the Father.

Thousands of years passed, and this Rose remains as it was when it first bloomed. Everyone who comes to see the Rose's beauty is changed. They smell His fragrance. They touch its soft petals. They bask in the Presence of the Rose. The Rose that will never die…..

Closer than a Brother

You, my Lord

Are closer to me

Than a brother

You are above all

There is no other

His Ways are not Our Ways

Is it raining or is God crying?
Although the rain provides nourishment
I wonder if each drop of rain
Are tears from God for our sins

His ways are not our ways
His thoughts are not our thoughts
They are higher, purer
He is full of light, full of wisdom
Full of love

We gave Him death, He gives us life
We gave Him a crown, but not of gold
We gave Him a robe, but in mockery

He is now wearing both the crown and robe
That we should have presented to Him
While He dwelt among us

One day we will see Him
Loved, clothed, honored and cherished

Then….our ways will be His ways
Then…our thoughts will be His
Then…our hearts will be one with Him

Kelly Taylor Nutt, Copyright © 1990

There is a Light

There is a Light
That shines on the nations

There is a Light
That shines on all the world

And although
There is great darkness

His love will penetrate
And chase away all fear

And although
All may seem hopeless

His love will resurrect
All who will hear

I am Calling for the One

I am calling for the one
The one who thinks
There is no hope for you

I'm calling to the one
The one who thinks
There is no way out

I am coming to
Bring My light to you

I am coming to
Chase the darkness away

Freedom is what
I am offering you

My power is stronger than...
What is holding you

So...

Come to Me
Come away with Me
Grab My hand when the enemy
Tries to pull you back

I am stronger than
What held you
My love
Will prevail

So...

Cling to Me
When the enemy
Fights for your soul

I am the One who
Bought you with a price

You are Mine
So let go

You are beautiful
Because I see
What you will be

When your heart
Is filled with Me

Birth Announcement!

Christmas is not all about presents
It is about a special birth
It is when God sent His Son
To live on the earth

Just as we can not wait to tell our family
About the birth of a son or daughter
God was just as excited
As mothers and fathers

We pick up the phone and make a call
Or tell those who are there
God sent angels to tell shepherds
Of His Son that He would share

We send beautiful announcements
Written on a card
God sent His announcement
In the form of a star

Angels! A star! Good news they bring!
Announcing to the world
The birth of our King!

KellyTaylor Nutt, Copyright © 2011

Blessed is His Name

Blessed be the Name of the Lord

Blessed be the Name of the Lord

Blessed be the Name of the Lord

For He is worthy

He is worthy

To be praised

Glorious is the Name of the Lord

Righteous is the Name of the Lord

Peace is the Name of the Lord

Love is the Name of the Lord

A myriad of names

Too numerous to condense into the contents of this page

Your Names, Oh Lord

Fill our hearts

As we praise and worship You!

Kelly Taylor Nutt, Copyright © 2016

To You Alone

To You, to You alone
To You alone we sing
To You, to You alone
I worship my King

You are our King
And I fall down before You
To You only we sing
We bow before You now

The King within our hearts
A King reigns there
A King, a mighty King
Won our hearts
The King for all eternity

You are our King
We worship You forever
You are our King
The King Who won our heart

You are the King
Who rules our lives forever
Take all of me
Every cell within my being

The Father

With my nose pressed against the window, I watched the family who lived across the street leave for church. I watched them laughing as their Daddy teased and threw them into the air. I was afraid he might miss and they would accidentally fall on the ground. But he caught them every time. "He is so strong", I thought. My eyes burned with tears as I watched them pull out of their driveway. Why didn't I have a Daddy? Why didn't my Mom take me to church? I knew she loved me, but she worked all of the time. How my heart ached to have someone throw me up and laugh with me.

My thoughts were interrupted as my teenage babysitter snarled and called my name with coldness. "You better get your room cleaned up!" she yelled. I complied, but it didn't change my thoughts. She must have been in a bad mood because everything I did or said made her angry. I finished cleaning my room and looked out of the window again.

I noticed the family across the street returning from church. My babysitter got angry again because there was so little food in the house. She started saying things about my Mom. That made me angry and I determined I would tell on her this time. She was still ranting as she spoke, "And another thing, your Mom didn't even buy bread!"

Suddenly, I had a thought. Not only could I escape her bad

mood, but I might get a smile from that Dad across the street. I asked her if I could borrow some bread from our neighbors. "Sure, knock yourself out," she replied.

I ran quickly across the street. I shyly rang the doorbell and waited. I was greeted by the Dad and his four children. I asked if I could borrow four pieces of bread. I knew Mom was getting paid today and that she would bring some groceries. The Dad said, "Sure, just a minute. I'll get some bread for you." I waited for what seemed like a long time. I noticed the kids with their noses pressed against the window as mine was earlier in the day. The Dad handed a bag to me. I told him thank you. I ran home, opened the bag and sat down.

When I looked in the bag, I noticed more than bread. He had added lunchmeat, cheese, potato chips and even candy. The babysitter seemed happy, and I was very excited about that. We ate until we were extremely full. She seemed to be better for the rest of the day. She had her moments, but, all in all, the atmosphere improved.

Weeks passed by and I spent more time with my new found friends. One day I heard some kids arguing. I ran outside because the neighborhood bully had stopped by to cause trouble. I ran over just as he was tauntingly saying, 'Well, my Dad is better than your Dad." Wrong choice of words. My friends lit into him with many words that were not very nice ones, to say the least. I was trying to stop the argument, so I spoke up. "I just wish I even had a Dad." With that, I turned around to walk home. One of my friends spoke saying, "I just wish I had a Mom." I turned to her and smiled. All of this time I had not realized I had not seen a Mom with them. I could not see past my own need to see theirs.

That Saturday, their Dad knocked at our door. He invited me and my Mom to church. Although Mom was reluctant, I jumped at the chance. The next day I was excited and scared all at the same time. I was going to church with them! While I was at church, I heard about a Heavenly Dad Who loved us, protected us, and wanted to spend time with us. I also learned that He had sent His own Son to die for us because He loved us so much. The pastor spoke of how our earthly Dad is in some ways a representative of our Heavenly Father. "Wow! I do have a Dad!", I thought. The pastor asked if anyone would like to meet Him and give their lives to Him. Conviction gripped me and I trusted my Heavenly Daddy with my whole heart.

When I got home, I told Mom about what happened to me at church. I told her about how I now had my own Dad. She seemed to listen, but not listen, if you know what I mean. My friends asked Mom if she wanted to go to Church again. She relented and went with us that night. The same thing that happened to me, happened to her!

The preacher said……and He is a Father to the fatherless. That is when my Mom broke. The Dad across the street put his arm around her and walked her to the front of the Church to meet her Heavenly Father, her Daddy, her Abba.

When she turned around, her whole face looked lighter and happier. She did not look as tired. I found out later that she also grew up without a Dad in her home. You can guess what happened next. Yep, they got married and the Dad across the street became my very own Dad. I got a double-deal! An earthly Dad and a heavenly Dad, which I already had, but just did not know about. No longer was the window smeared where my nose used to be. No longer was I lonely for a Dad.

And to top it off, my friends became my brothers and sisters. My life was fantastic!

When the bully came by to cause his weekly trouble, I was ready. When he tauntingly said, "Look at the boy without a Dad!" I was ready for him. I told him that I have two Dads now and that I have the best Dad of all. I told him all about Him. I told him that He was his Heavenly Father too, whether he liked it or not. I saw him change a little when he heard that. Every week I kept telling him about the best Dad in the world. Finally, he came to church with us after I kept talking to him for months. And the same thing that happened to my Mom and me, happened to him. "This is too cool!" I thought.

And my babysitter? She is next.

His Love

His love was stronger than the cross.

His love was larger than what He
knew He would go through.

His love for His Father, His love for us

Led Him to climb the hill
that lead to His death.

His love caused Him to answer
the question the Pharisees asked.

Fully aware that His answer would
be the deciding factor of His fate.

"I adjure you, by the Living God,
tell us if You are the Messiah,
the Son of the Living God."

Without hesitation, He truthfully
answered and proclaimed....

"**I AM.** And you will see Me
seated at the right hand of the Father."

He knew that they would accuse Him
of blasphemy.

He knew that the punishment for blasphemy
was....

DEATH.

He knew, yet He answered.

His love answered their question.

Empty

The manger was empty when the soldiers tried to kill Him

The tomb was empty when the soldiers tried to find Him.

Where did He go?

We know!

He is seated on His throne
And resides within our hearts.

Empty manger. Empty tomb. Empty hearts.

NOW FILLED!

The Precious Gift

We wrap our gift with ribbons and bows
God wrapped His gift in swaddling clothes

We give gifts to our family
God gave the gift to set us free

We tear our gifts to see what is inside
God tore the veil when Jesus died

We search for the right gift for those we love
God sent the perfect gift from above

God looks to and fro on the earth to see
Who will accept His gift and be set free

Salvation is as easy as opening a gift on Christmas day
The only difference is, this gift will not go away

This gift of Jesus will be with you all year long
He will never leave or forsake you
Because to Him you will belong

Rip open your heart
Receive God's gift to you

You are not just receiving,

The Precious Gift

You are giving a gift too

He will cherish your heart
Just as you will cherish Him living there

He will change you, He will love you
He will take every care

'No gift on earth is greater
Receive His gift today
No love was every greater
Than when He gave His life away!

Who is this Man?

From my house in Jerusalem
I saw a man come to our town
He sat upon a donkey
The people bowing to the ground
Placing branches before Him
Crying, *"Blessed is He,*
Who comes in the name of the Lord!"

As He came into Jerusalem
I questioned, "Who is this man?"
He healed the lame
And restored a withered hand
Who is this man?
Who sees peoples' needs
As no one else can
Who is He, I don't understand?"

This same man who did so much
For many people in my town
I now see struggling with a cross
And on His head a crown
But not a crown as I expected
They must have the wrong man
Who is He? I don't understand

As I stood near the cross

Who is this Man?

With many people from my town
In disbelief I watched
As His blood fell to the ground
"Surely this was the Son of God",
Proclaimed one man
Who is He, who is this man?

As I grew and got older
I continued to search for a clue
Why did He have to die?
What wrong did He do?
Then someone showed me a passage
From the prophecy
Isaiah, spoke clearly to me

He was wounded for our transgressions
And bruised for our iniquities
By His stripes we are healed
He bore our sorrows and our griefs
His Name is Immanuel, Immanuel
Now I understand
And I know....

He was more than a man

The Best of the Best

The best of the best

From the east to the west

The best of the best

The best of the blessed

The best teacher

The best preacher

The best singer

The best writer

The best King

The best God

The best offering

Our best friend

The Best of the Best

Jesus Christ, voted Best all Around
for 2000+ years in a row

Actually, for all eternity

But for the sake of the poem
We will begin with His appearance
On earth

The Lion Roars

The earth shakes
As the Lion roars
Out of Zion
We hear the sound
Of Jesus roaring
Calling to the nations
"Come unto Me
I will lead you through the jungle.
You do not have to fear.
For I am King of the jungle.
I am King of the nations.
I am King over all the earth."

Listen to the sounds
Listen to the sounds
Listen to the sounds of the jungle
As the King declares His dominion
Listen as He cries out for His people
Listen as He roars a song of love
To the nations

Do you hear Him roar?
Do you feel the earth shake?
Do you see Him standing on the mountain?
Do you feel His heart
As it breaks

For the nations?

With one breath He shakes the heavens
With one touch He causes healing
With one word He brings deliverance
Listen to the sounds He is revealing

Yes, I hear Him roar
I feel the earth shake
I see Him standing on the mountain
I can feel His heart as it breaks
For the nations

We proclaim that You are King
We guard Your territory
We overcome as we sing
See Him standing in His glory

Listen to the sound
Listen to the sound
Listen to the sound.

Shhh! Listen!

How Many Drops of Blood

How many drops of blood
Did it take to provide
Full forgiveness for
Restoration for
All mankind?

How many drops of blood
Fell to earth to cleanse the world?
The drops of blood that fell
From a sinless Lamb
Only these drops of blood can cleanse
Every person from their sins
The worthy sacrifice
Was Jesus Christ
For this purpose He came to the world

If the voice of Abel's blood
Cried out from the ground
How much more did Jesus' blood
Cry to the Father
Abel was killed by his own
Also, Jesus died alone
Abel's sacrifice was acceptable
But only Christ's can atone

Surely He has borne our griefs and carried our sorrow

How Many Drops of Blood

Yet we did esteem Him smitten of God and afflicted
Wounded for our transgression
And bruised for our iniquities
The chastisement of our peace was upon Him
With His stripes we are healed
A Lamb lead to die
The Son of God revealed
But rejected

It should have been us on the cross
But we could not pay the price
There was only One, a Holy One
A sinless sacrifice
Who was free from all sin
The blood that flowed from Him
Was extraordinary

Holy blood
Blood able to cleanse....

Us all

Forever His Word

Forever is the Word of God written in my heart
Forever it has changed my life
It will always be a part
Of my life, my thoughts, my hopes and my dreams
It is the living Word and every day it seems
To become more alive to me
Changing motives, thoughts and ways
That seemed okay to me
To the Word I give my praise

Jesus is the Word of God Who came into my heart
Forever He has changed my life
He will always be a part
Of my life, my thoughts, my hopes and my dreams
He is the Living Word and every day He seems
To become more alive to me
Changing motives, thoughts and ways
That seemed okay to me
To Him, I give my praise

No other book in all the world
Can change peoples' lives
If you wonder why it is unique
So many years survived

Because every Word was inspired by God

Forever His Word

The Author is our Creator
No where can such a book be found
With truths any greater

Jesus is the Word of God
Who will come into your heart
Forever He will change your life
If you ask and do your part

He will not intrude, you must invite Him in
Oh, the peace that He will bring
Read His Word today.....

There you will find your King

The Groom

One day when I was a teenager I lay on my bed. My diary was in my hand. I was thinking of all the characteristics I would like to see in my future husband. I took my pen and began to write them down. I was very tired, so I put the pen and diary down and began day-dreaming of my Groom. Sleep overtook my thoughts. I began to dream. In the dream, God the Father appeared to me. He said, "I'd like to introduce My Son to you. "

On the right side of the throne, I saw a man standing there. I could only see His back at first. He was dressed in a purple robe and a crown was on His head. He looked majestic, even though I had yet to see His face. Slowly He turned around. Glory followed Him like a swirl. Clothed in unimaginable glory, I saw His face.

The first thing I noticed was the most beautiful eyes I had ever seen. Love poured out of them. In one glance, I saw all of the characteristics I desired in a man. Compassion, love, jealousy, conviction, strength and protection could be seen and felt. My eyes were locked on His. A swirl of emotion permeated my very being. How could one look from His eyes change me in an instant? I remember thinking, when I get back down to earth, I'm going to write in my diary about this Man I just met. But as I continued thinking, I realized there would be no possible way to describe Someone Who is so vast and indescribable. It would be impossible to condense everything about Him with just a pen and a piece of paper.

The Father began to speak and my attention was solely on Him. He joyfully explained all that Jesus had done for me and would do for me in the future. All He would require is for me to give my heart to Him. He explained how He had been willing to leave His position in Heaven so He could redeem all of mankind. He told me how He had been born in a manger without a lot of fanfare. He explained in detail how He had given His life for mine. The Father continued with stories of how pure and holy His Son was, and although He was tempted to sin, He did not. Because of His great love for the Father and us, He laid down His life. He then spoke lovingly to His Son. *"This is my beloved Son, in Who I am well pleased."*

After the Lord finished speaking, I had a time of reflection. The Father reminded me of my own Dad in some ways. I remember how my Dad was showing some of my accomplishments to his friends. Then he began showing pictures of me at difference stages of my life. After the pictures, he brought out the blue ribbons. I was kind of embarrassed about all of the attention I was getting, but at the same time, I liked knowing how much my earthly Dad loved me. I wondered if that was what Jesus was thinking as He heard His Father speaking so highly of Him.

The next thing I felt and noticed was the vast difference in Jesus and me. I felt so ashamed and dirty compared to the purity and holiness I saw. I cried as I understood what Jesus had done for me. I asked the Father, "How can I join Him

47

as His bride?" I'm so sinful and He is so pure. There is no comparison between us. The Father explained further. "Jesus has seen you and chosen you." "Me? Why?"

It was then that Jesus spoke. "May I answer?" It was the first time I heard His voice. All of the qualities I saw in His eyes matched what I heard in His voice. He said, "You see, child, I was tempted in the very same way you were tempted. I saw you when you laughed, when you cried, when you rebelled, and when you sinned. I saw everything, but My love for you is unconditional, steadfast, never-changing or never-ending. I saw what you would become if you allowed Me to come into your heart and change it. You are beautiful in My eyes, although you can not see yourself the way I do. You look in the mirror and see someone you hate at times. But I look in the same mirror and the reflection I see is quite different. Because when I come to dwell inside of you, you will begin to change from glory to glory. I gave My life for yours so that you could live with Me forever.

I was speechless. The only sound that came from me were sobs as I understood what He was trying to explain to me. I bowed down and confessed my sins before Him. I desired more than anything for Him to live inside of my heart. And I asked Him to come and do just that. Immediately He came to me, embraced and comforted my heart. A deep cleansing took place in my spirit. I felt His peace surround me. I felt His glory cover me. I knew I was His. We turned to the Father. He was smiling. We were smiling. The angels were rejoicing. Love swirled all around us.

I woke up from my dream and realized it had been more than a dream. I fell to the floor, repented and again asked Jesus to come into my heart.

I picked my diary and pen up and began to write. I wrote, Today, I met the man I have longed for all of my life. I know everyone has their own unique ways of sharing Jesus with a world which is sometimes hostile to the idea that such a man exists. Much less a man Who was born for, lived for, died for and was resurrected for each one of us. And He wants us to be born again, live for Him, die to ourselves and be resurrected as He was. But I know that He is real and I want to share Him with you. I will continue to write of Him all the days of my life.

My Groom wants to be yours as well. Do you want Him?

The Sound of Your Voice

No television or movie
Or other distracting noise

Direct me and focus me
Because I'm listening for
The sound of Your voice

It is quiet now
Breathe on me
Touch my heart
And set me free

I will be listening for
The sound of Your voice

Oh, the things that clutter
The clamoring sounds
There is always a noise
So quietly I will turn around

From distractions

The Sound of Your Voice

And screaming noise
And still my heart
As I listen for the sound of Your voice

Oh, Your soothing voice
That still small voice
Your voice is what I long for

I Can Not Wait!

I can not wait to touch Your face
Your face that was marred
I can not wait to see Your face
Your face that was scarred

I can not wait to see Your eyes
Outpouring compassion and love
I can not wait to look into them
You have eyes of a dove

I can not wait to touch Your hands
The hands that were torn
I can not wait to see the hands
That touched the forlorn

I can not wait to see You wearing the robe
And crown You deserved
The King Who gave everything
The King Who healed and served

I can not wait to see You Jesus
I can not wait to see You!
I can not wait to be with You forever
When You make all things new!

I Love You For

I love You for the words
That come out of Your mouth
And the love that comes
Out of Your heart
I love You for the strength
That comes out of Your arms
Keeping me safe from harm

I love You for the peace
That comes from Your touch
And the love that shines
Out of Your eyes
I love You because
You love me so much
Hearing all my cries

I love You for the kindness
You show me
As it leads me to repent
I love You because You set me free
And for the Son You sent

I love You for the blood You shed
And the hope You put in my heart
I love You because
We will soon be wed
Never to be apart

I love You…I love You…I love You!

The Bride

Here is the bride's rendition of what happened on one of the evenings she spent with her Groom.

Passionately I wait for the appearance of the One my soul loves. My clothes were pressed, repaired and clean. All the stains had been washed away by my Groom. My daily work, interruptions and distractions were set aside as I prepared for His arrival. I had scheduled my evening time to spend with Him. A time to be spent together just talking and enjoying each other's presence. I always learn more about His character, His desires and what He needs to change within me so I can become more like Him.

As I waited for Him, I remembered how I had learned not to allow the cares of the world entangle me and cause me to miss this special time with Him. I had learned that He did not care if I used eloquent words or prayed using the right formula. I remembered how I had come to the realization that He was simply and overwhelmingly in love with me. I also had learned if I would but whisper His name, He was right there, listening to my every word. He was more concerned that I would get to know Him better.

Soon, I heard a sound. My heart pounded, my hands were perspiring as I walked toward the sound. My soul panted, just as a deer who pants for water. Look! There He is, standing behind our wall, gazing through the windows, peering through the lattice. Listen! He is knocking. I saw His hand as it reached through the latch-opening. As I opened the door, Jesus entered, smiling with pure joy. I stood there admiring His countenance. His love was more delightful to me than wine. His name is like perfume poured out. I delighted to sit in His shade. His fruit is sweet to my taste. Everything about Him is pure. Holy. Righteous. I am faint from love.

He then came and put His arms around me. He spoke, "How beautiful you are. Oh, how beautiful. Your eyes are doves. You have stolen my heart with one glance of your eyes. You are Mine, and I am yours." He then swung me around in a circle and began singing over me. His left arm was under my head, and His right arm embraced me. He said, "Let Me hear your voice, for your voice is sweet." So I began to sing back to Him as we danced around the room. I held on to Him and would not let Him go. He then said, "Come away with Me." Away we ran as He leaped across the mountains, bounded over the hills, and guided me in the paths of righteousness. He lead me to a river with still waters. He made me lie down in a green pasture. I will not fear evil, because He was with Me. As I lay there, looking at the beautiful stars He created, He teasingly said, "I would ask you how your day was, but I already know!" I felt laughter bubbling up in my spirit. I began laughing and could not stop. Joy filled my soul, and the seemingly large problems I faced that day melted away. Oh, how I loved Him!! He knew my heart was completely free from distractions that would draw my attention away from Him. My focus was now completely on Him. He always made time for me, His bride. And I realized that nothing could ever separate me from His love.

I could not stop the worship that rose from my heart. Jesus, I love You. Your kindness always leads me to repentance. Your holiness and purity and righteousness are untouchable. There is none like You. You died for me. You gave everything so I can receive everything. You were resurrected so I can rest in assurance that I, too, will be raised as You were. Everything about You is good. You have set me free. You have washed me with Your blood. You are above all. You are Lord of Lords and King of Kings. Your banner over me is LOVE. I continued worshiping as I watched how pleased He was to hear true praise rising up from within me.

So many had cursed Him today, so I hoped it was refreshing for Him to hear me speak about why I was so in love with Him. He then asked me if I would like Him to read a love story to me. He beckoned me to sit on His lap, just as a child would sit in its Father's lap to listen to a bedtime story.

He opened the Bible and turned to the Song of Solomon and read it to me. He would read to me the parts that were His parts, then He had me read my parts in the story. It was like He had written it just for me. When we got to the last chapter, chapter 8, He focused on verse 6-7. He said, Memorize this, because when it truly gets into your heart, your spirit, it becomes a part of you. It describes in detail My abundant love for you, My sister, My spouse.

We began reading this verse together. PLACE ME LIKE A SEAL OVER YOUR HEART, LIKE A SEAL ON YOUR ARM;

FOR LOVE IS AS STRONG AS DEATH, ITS JEALOUSY UNYIELDING AS THE GRAVE. IT BURNS LIKE BLAZING FIRE, LIKE A MIGHTY FLAME. MANY WATERS CANNOT QUENCH LOVE; RIVERS CANNOT WASH IT AWAY. IF ONE WERE TO GIVE ALL THE WEALTH OF HIS HOUSE FOR LOVE, IT WOULD BE UTTERLY SCORNED. Song of Solomon 8:6-7 NIV.

After we finished reading His love story, it was time to go home. I secretly wished He had made days longer than twenty-four hour periods, because I would rather be with Him than sleep. Knowing my thoughts, He replied, "Soon beloved, soon. My bride......time will not matter any more."

The Unforgiven Diamond

Feeling desperate and all alone, the woman who had been caught in adultery faced her punishment. She had been despised by all who knew her. Her life was filled with sin, mistakes and condemnation. No matter how many times she tried to fix herself up to look and act presentable, the townspeople remembered. It was hard enough for her to forgive herself, but their contempt and scorn made it impossible.

She tried to enter into conversation with the local women, but was met with silence, glances of judgment and sometimes verbal confrontations.

Even when she apologized with tears that burned her eyes, they remained unmoved.

When she gave gifts or gave of herself in an act of kindness, her actions were ignored.

Consumed by the rejection and self-hatred that overwhelmed her, and coupled with the community's response, she gave up.

She no longer cared what she did, or how much pain it would eventually cause her.

Yet now, she faced death. She knew that within hours, she would be surrounded by people with large stones. She understood that the rocks would be hurled at her, one after the other. She knew she would die.

She secretly was ready anyway. Why should she want to continue to live when all who knew her hated her?

It was not that hard to leave the house full of loneliness, isolation and emptiness. It was not that difficult to shut the door as she headed toward her punishment.

She walked with her head down and did not look into the eyes of angry, gossiping women.

The men violently grabbed her and walked with her to the place where she would be killed. The Pharisees and the teachers of the law continued to treat her roughly until they stopped.

It was then that she looked up and saw a man sitting there. His countenance was unlike anyone she had ever seen before. He did not stare back with hatred as the men who brought her there did.

The Pharisees said His name, followed by a question.

She had heard His name a week ago. She had overheard some women speaking unfavorably about Him as she walked past them to draw water.

What she saw at this moment, did not match how they described Him.

She also remembered His name when others were speaking favorably about Him. She thought about going to hear Him, but remembered other religious leaders, and decided against it. She wanted nothing to do with another religious guy.

Her accusers asked Jesus this question. "This woman was caught in the act of adultery. The law of Moses says to stone her. What do you say?"

The woman saw Jesus bend down. Thinking that He was bending down to pick up a rock, she closed her eyes. She was anxiously waiting to feel a stone hit her in the skull, but that did not happen.

She opened her eyes back up, and saw that Jesus was writing something in the sand with His finger.

Perplexed, she questioned what He was doing.

It was then that He answered their question. He said, "He who is without sin, let him cast the first stone." The woman was stunned by the answer and shocked at their response.

Her accusers left her, one by one. Their rocks were thrown on the ground instead of at her.

The only one left was Jesus. He asked her, "Woman, where are your accusers? Didn't even one of them condemn you?" She answered, "No, Lord." "Neither do I; Go, and sin no more," Jesus replied.

The woman sat in awe after Jesus left. She was attempting to comprehend what happened. She not only stopped sinning, but this unforgiven diamond followed Him. He gave her love that she had never known before.

This hidden diamond had been buried deeply within the earth's surface. Surrounded by a dark substance called coal, she was ignored. She was brought to the surface and noticed by the Forgiver. As she laid on the ground before her accusers, she was exposed for all to see. What they saw was the dark black outer portion of who she was.

The Master saw beyond her darkness. He could see the diamond within. He knew who she would become when He added His brilliant light that would shine within her.

This once-dirty rock had been transformed into a beautiful forgiven diamond, full of hope. Every day she changed as she listened to the words that nourished her soul. Every day His colors began to shine brighter within her as His light radiated into her heart.

She was now a beautiful forgiven diamond. Full of life. Full of light. Full of hope. Full of color.

For she was now a reflection of the King Who lived within her heart.

No Abuse

Jesus will not:
>Use me
>Abuse me
>Refuse me
>Accuse me
>or
>Confuse me

But He did:
>Choose me
>Amuse me
>And
>He will not
>Lose me

The Path

Wherever the Lord walks, a trail of love follows. He walks on the city streets. The busy highway becomes a highway of holiness when He travels there. This is where the story begins.

A man is leaning against a wall in a half-sitting position. An empty bottle of liquor is still in his hand. This bottle is one of a few things he has left. No home. No car. No job. No wife. No children. All have turned away from him in scorn. So, his days are spent finding ways to make just enough money to buy another bottle of wine. When he gets enough money to buy one, his soul is satisfied. But his spirit remains empty. He can not explain the emptiness that consumes him. This wine takes him out of the reality of the day. With a bottle he finds some sort of comfort.

Jesus stopped as He saw this broken man. He looked on him with fierce love in His eyes. "Oh, my son, turn to me. Turn from the pain, the sin, and the path that has brought you to this place. Turn from your ways and follow Me. My path leads you to life. Wherever I walk, love follows. Whoever I touch, love penetrates and breaks through their hardened, broken heart."

The Lord sees someone approaching. With mischief and scorn in their hearts, they came to take what little possessions this man has left. He awakens and watches as they take his wallet full of memories of the life he once knew. The tear-stained pictures he treasured were stolen. Helpless, he laid there because no strength was left to fight. They carelessly threw the wallet in the trash, not knowing they had taken everything from a man who had nothing. The man began to cry. Jesus, seeing his pain, wept with him.

The Lord sees someone else approaching. He had seen what happened. He walked past the man and picked up his wallet. Gently he placed the wallet back into his hand. The man began crying again. "Thank you," he slurred. Surprised by this man's kindness, he asked why he had done this for him. The man replied, "Because where you are now, I once was. I too had chosen the path that leads to destruction. I too had a dirty concrete sidewalk as my bed. Alley cats were my friends. What I thought were my true friends had left, one by one. Oh, they had come down the path with me for awhile, but turned around when the thorns grew thicker. This path was wide and easy to follow, at first."

It started out with fun. Partying became my reason for living. But days of partying turned into years. Oversleeping and missing work became a weekly occurrence. Soon I lost my job. Then another and another. Then I lost something more important than a job. I lost my wife. She said she could not live with the man I had become. She took my kids and started over.

I now was so far down on this path that I could not find my way back. The path that began with fun, had become a dark, lonely place. Thorns and briar-patches followed me at every turn. Overgrowth of weeds surrounded me. I finally gave up trying to find my way back to the fork in the road, where I had turned the wrong way. It was impossible to find my way back on my own. Although I blamed everyone and everything, I realized that ultimately, I was the one who kept walking when many people begged me to turn around.

I knew I needed help, but I had no idea where that help would come from. One night a man came to me, just as I am coming to you. He told me of a Man who can lead me back through the thorns, briar-patches and back to the fork in the road. He told me He would walk with me as I turn down the right path. He said it would be easy at first because He would cut down the weeds. He would help me jump over the obstacles that stood in my way.

This path is paved with love, filled with light and full of peace. When it gets too rough, He will lie down in green pastures with you. He will refresh your feet in the still waters. He will guide you to His path of righteousness for His name sake. He will remove you from the wilderness and take you to the promised land.

This broken-hearted man asked, "Who is this man? How can I meet Him?" "His name is Jesus. He is right here. Waiting to pierce your heart with His love. You just need to ask Him to come into your heart and repent for turning onto the destructive path." he replied.

The homeless man bowed his head and cried out to Jesus. Right then, Jesus' love poured in his heart. Jesus stepped in and drove the enemy out. He took him by the hand and they started walking down the path that leads to eternal life. A path with flowers soaked in love. A path where the leaves of the trees were full of healing. The dust on the ground turned to gold as they continued walking. He found more treasures along this path. Under a rock he found restoration. He turned over the next rock and under it he found joy, then hope. The path was strewn with the attributes of God that He wanted to build in this new man. Peace, patience, kindness, goodness, mercy and gentleness were found along the way.

His burden was gone. His chains were broken. He continued to follow Jesus' every step. As he grew stronger, the time came when the Lord lead him to return to the place where he first found Jesus. He looked down and saw another man sleeping with a bottle in his hand. He took the bottle and replaced it with a Bible. Suddenly, the man stirred and began cursing at him. Unfazed, He replied, "Can I tell you a story? Jesus smiled as He watched. And the story continues…….. one wins one, who then wins another, who then wins another. And it will continue until the King returns.

Not One Tear

Not one tear that falls that I do not catch it
Not one hair that falls that I do not count it
Not one step you take will be without Me
Child, I know you

Not one sin that I do not see it
Not one sin that I will not forgive it
Not one thing will make me go away
Child, I forgive you

Not any pain so deep that I can not feel it
Not any mountain that I can not melt it
No one will stand in our way
Child, I will lead you

No one else loves me like Jesus!
No one else knows me like Him!
No one else can feel my heartbeat!
Not anyone but Him!

Let there be Light!

The earth was formless and void
And covered with darkness
But the Spirit of God
Moved upon the face
The face of the waters
Then He brought forth light
And He brought forth life
BOOM....A new creation!

Our lives were formless and void
And covered with darkness
But the Spirit of God
Moved upon our lives
He sent conviction
He brought forth sight
He brought forth light
BOOM....A new creation!

Our lives are now filled with His Light
And no more covered with darkness
Because the Spirit of God
Moved in our lives
And brought revelation

He brought forth light
He brought forth life
BOOM….We are a new creation!

Boom, boom, boom….Salvation!
Boom, boom, boom….A new creation!
Boom, boom, boom….Revelation!
Boom, boom, boom….Restoration!

Basket of Burdens

As we walk around on the earth, we as people tend to pick up burdens that are too heavy to carry. Circumstances become burdens when we allow them to stay in our hearts and lives too long.

Instead of giving them to the Lord, we sometimes hold onto them.

I see the Lord reaching down into this basket full of burdens that are weighing us down and bending us over. He picks up the basket easily, and we are able to stand straight with His strength as we release the basket into His arms. Although many times we try to hold on to the basket, and not let Him carry it for us.

A few years ago, my basket of burdens was full, and it was weighing me down. It was as if He was trying to take the basket from me and I was using all of my strength and fighting Him as He was attempting to pry it from my hands.

He is stronger than I am, so He helped me release the contents inside the basket and put it on His shoulders instead of mine. He took me close to His side, and we kept walking as I leaned into my Beloved's arms.

His Word says, *"Casting all your cares upon Him, for He cares for you."* 1 Peter 5:7.

So Father, I release to You any burdens that I may have picked up again.

I pray for everyone reading this. Many are carrying loads that they cannot possibly handle. Thank You that You are willing to carry them for us, and even carry us, through the hard times. Jesus, thank You again for dying for us. You took all of our sin, all of our burdens, and You Lord, can handle anything. I trust You today. In Jesus name, amen.

Let My People Go!

Let
My
People
Go!

Many many years ago
There was a man named Pharoah
Who held God's people as slaves
They needed to be saved
The people cried in agony
"Father God, set us free!"
In response to their cries
Moses was sent with God's reply
As He cried out

"Let My People Go!"

Two thousand years ago
Remained the spirit of Pharoah
Throughout all of history
People need Someone to set them free
The people cried, "Free us!"
God sent His Son Jesus
Free us from our sin!
His response is the same now
As it was then

"Let…My…People…Go!"

In our day a sound is heard
His people speak the same words
"Father God, set us free!"
And I believe in the heavenlies
God is heard above all the sounds
As His voice thunders down

"Let…My…People…Go!"

The Filthy Rags

Donned in high heels, short skirt, tight shirt and jewelry I looked into the full-length mirror. "What guy can resist this?," I pondered. As I walked to school that morning I heard cat-calls and whistles coming from passing cars. I saw men looking in their rear-view mirrors. Just as I was feeling pretty good about myself, a car drove by. The car was full of teenage boys. Thinking that I would receive more looks, I flipped my hair back, smiled and looked their way. But instead of hearing more "compliments", I heard four-letter obscenities and propositions that I can not even tell anyone about.

In shame and humiliation, I turned and ran home. When I got there, I looked in the mirror again. I did not see the same person I saw before. Maybe the neckline of my shirt was too low. Maybe my skirt was too high. But I began reasoning. I knew I was not what they said I was. The others thought I was pretty. So I decided not to change my attire and walk to school again. As I was walking, a car stopped. The cutest guy I have ever seen stared at me through the window. With a nice grin on his face he asked if I would like a ride to school.

Normally I would not have accepted, but I knew him. He was in my 3rd hour history class and I had a huge crush on him. So I accepted the ride. We began talking and time flew by. We pulled into the parking lot. Before I got out, he touched my arm and said, "I think you are beautiful." I felt my face flush and looked away from him. Then I looked back into his eyes and said thank you.

 I was relieved that I had not changed my clothes. I decided from that moment on, I would continue to dress like I did that day. He asked for my phone number, called me every day and we became inseparable. The more time we were together, the more I knew in my heart that I wanted to grow old with him.

The day came when he looked me in the eyes and told me he loved me. He gave me my first kiss as I melted in his arms. Our relationship progressed until one day, I made a very important decision. A very wrong decision. I will spare you the details.

 Soon after I had allowed this, I looked in the mirror again. I did not like what I saw. I felt like I had become what those teenage boys had called me. My boyfriend started acting differently and stopped calling. One day I saw him drive by with another girl sitting closely to him.

In retaliation, I began flirting with other guys. I hoped that would change his heart and he would come running back to me. When that did not happen, I started other relationships and gave to them what I had given away to him. I got a lot of attention and a lot of " I love you's." But with each passing day as I looked in the mirror, I did not like the reflection. Oh, I looked good on the outside. But within, I felt so dirty, used and abandoned.

I felt like the beautiful clothes were filthy rags.

One morning, I was again walking to school. My attire had not changed. A car slowed down and stopped. I was thinking, "Oh no, here we go again." A teenager started speaking to me and told me something I had never heard before. He told me that Jesus loved me. He told me that He died for my sins. I remember thinking that I did not sin. How could anybody love me anyway? But when I looked into his eyes, they sparkled with some sort of light.

I had heard about how Christians judge people so much, but I did not feel any judgment coming from him at all. He placed an invitation in my hand that told more about the church service. The service was to be held that night. All day I fought within myself. I finally decided to give it a shot. I remembered the last time some guy told me he loved me.

As I dressed that evening, I thought I better dress more appropriately. I was nervous, but I did not let it show. My heart had become hardened.

When I got to church, the people were smiling, raising their hands and swaying to the music. It was like they were dancing. How could they love this Jesus they were singing about. He will just use, abuse and leave them. I was fighting tears and the feelings I was having. To keep my mind off the songs, I imagined I was at a prom. Dressed in
A gorgeous blue dress, I waited......

The Dance

I was sitting on a chair in the ballroom. Feeling somewhat rejected, I watched as one young girl after another was asked to join in a dance. I remember thinking, "Maybe my dress is too ugly. Maybe I'm ugly!" I lowered my head toward the floor.

It was then that I saw a pair of sandled feet standing in front of me. I raised my head and looked up. My eyes met the eyes of pure love. It was Jesus! With His hand extended toward me, He beckoned, "Would you like to dance?" My head dropped again because I felt unworthy to be asked by such a One.

Thoughts flooded my heart. "Why would He choose me? I have lived such a terrible life!" Past sins continued to creep into my mind. But I sensed Him speaking to me as each sin was revealed. He said, "That sin was covered by My blood when I died for you."

What do you do when such Holiness is standing in front of you? I began weeping and asking Him to forgive me for what I did. There were so many sins that I finally blurted out, "Jesus, forgive me for all of them!" "I feel so unworthy to dance with You." He replied, "My desire is to live within your heart so I can change it." In response to His overwhelming love and kindness I cried out, "Forgive me! Come into my heart! Change me!"

Immediately, I sensed peace and a deep cleansing that is hard to explain. Joy abounded in my heart. I took His hand as He stood me up and began leading me in a dance. I heard angels rejoicing and He was singing a song to me that was so beautiful, it took my breath away. He sang, The Lord God is with you, He is mighty to save. He will take great delight in you, He will quiet you with His love, He will rejoice over you with singing. *(Zeph. 3:17)*.

I felt clumsy as we stepped out. I was worried that I would step on His beautiful feet. Those feet that I noticed standing before me awhile ago. But the more we danced, the easier it became to trust His every step.

I could not control my admiration. I worshiped Him as I spoke. "Your eyes are so full of love, so full of compassion. Your mouth speaks the truth. Your ears hear the very thoughts of my heart. Your arms are full of strength and just one touch brings healing to every area of my heart.

Then He broke loose and began spinning around and around. He spoke His Word from *Zephaniah 3:17* again. He continued, "You are beautiful to Me as well. You are no longer blinded by the god of the world. How great is My love for you My child! You now understand that I created you. I died for you and was raised so that you can have assurance that you can live with Me forever. My hands of protection surround you. Nothing can separate you from My love."

But if someone from your past comes along, and tries to take you away, I will have to let you go. The choice is yours. But remember that My desire is that you remain in My arms forever." I exclaimed, "How overjoyed I am that I accepted Your invitation to dance Jesus!" My head rested on His shoulder. His glory covered me and I again saw His feet. I knelt down and my tears covered them. I wiped them with my hair.

As He stood me up He said, "May I have the next dance as well?" What could I say? "Of course You can Jesus!" I shouted. This time, I did not drop my head in shame. Because He had released me from that. We continued to dance until I got tired. He then walked me home. I climbed into bed as He covered me with His presence. "Good night Lord," I whispered. "I love You." He teasingly replied, "I loved you first." We both smiled, and I drifted off to sleep. I thought He left, and didn't realize it, but He stayed while I slept. He continued His song that He sang over me. For the first time in my life, I slept in peace, not even knowing that He never left my side.

Children of the Light

Children of the night
Children of the night
Everywhere
Children of the night
Will be children
Of the Light
When they turn

I am drawing them unto Myself
I am drawing them to My Light
I am drawing them to
My arms of love
Now Children of the Light

Children of the light
Children of the light
Come!

I will make a way
Where there is no way
I will light your footsteps
Along the way

Children of the night
Will overcome with My Light
When they come

I will lead you by the still waters
I will comfort your soul
No more turmoil
Fills your heart now
For I have made you whole

I will wrap My arms around you
I will help you see the Light
For I am love, and I am light
I make the darkness bright

I will comfort you when you are broken
I will comfort you when you fear
When the ground shakes
I will touch your heart
You will know that
I am always near

I am drawing you to Myself
I will chase you
I will show you My love
In a myriad of ways
I love you

I will pour my Spirit upon you
And your heart will be changed
I will see that you are taken care of
Your life re-arranged

Come to Me when you are weary
Come to Me when you are tired
I save all your tears in a bottle
Your heart is what I require

Come to Me when you are thirsty
Come to Me when you are dry
I will feed you when you need more
I am the One you are searching for

The craving in your heart
Will be filled to over-flowing
And I will set you free
On the cross, with My blood
I won you for all eternity

I gave you My life
On the cross
I saw you in the future
And I didn't want you
Apart from Me

Yes, I saw you in the future

I said, "I want that one!"
At the cross, the enemy defeated
Victory was won....

When I took My last breath

Children of the night
Now children of My Light

All

All who desire to see Me...

will see Me

All who seek Me...

will find Me

All who desire to hear Me...

will hear Me

All who desire to know Me

will know Me.

And I WILL give you the desires of your heart.

Do Not Soil What I've Cleansed

Do not soil what I have cleansed
Do not remind Me of what I have forgotten
Do not let condemnation drown you
Do not let judgment cover you
Do not dig up what I have buried
Do not pick up burdens that are not Mine
Do not carry weights only I can carry
I will carry them for you

For you are the weaker vessel
I am strong
You are not equipped to carry them
Place your burdens on My shoulders

Let only My voice lead you
Let My blood cleanse you
Let My righteousness clothe you
Let My forgiveness cover you
Let My peace surround you
Let My light guide you
Let darkness flee from you
Let My Word change you
Let My reflection shine in your eyes
Let My Spirit arise in you
Let Me take over…

Kelly Taylor Nutt, Copyright © 2011

86

My Tears Fell

My tears fell from my eyes
I kiss Your feet with my lips
My sin not disguised
You saw it
I dried Your feet with my hair
My love I shared
I did not care who saw it

I danced before My Lord
In front of the crowd
I did not despise
My Father
As I twirled around
My wife frowned
As I showed my love
To my Father

Our love we show
So the world will know
That we love Someone
Named Jesus
We do not care
If people stare

As we express our love
To Jesus

Whatever we do, to show Your love
To a world in need of a Saviour
We will not be ashamed
We will not hide in fear
We will shout His Name
To all who will hear

All He Requires

God desires a willing, obedient heart
To do what He wants to do through you
All He requires is a yielded spirit
To accomplish His work in you
You may think you have no talent
But that is not true
The Omnipotent One
Who created the entire universe
Created only one you

God also desires your heart to be....
A place for Him to rest
A place for Him to dwell
So filled with an overwhelming love for Him
That it bursts and His love spills out

Oh, He so wants to use you!
No talent is too small
Do not let the enemy accuse you
Give Jesus your all

You may think that no one loves you
But that is not true

God, Who created the universe
Wants me to tell you

That He truly loves you
And He certainly does care
He so wants to use you
Your burdens He will bear
And He is strong enough
To lift the burdens off your shoulders
And place them on His

Casting all of your cares on Him, for He cares for you!
1 Peter 5:7

Come and Get Me

The Lord presents
His peace to you
It is yours

Come and get it!

With open hand
He places it in your soul

Do you want it?

He will place peace
In your soul
Change your heart
And make you whole
Be immersed in His love

Come and Get Me!

His hand of blessing
Is holding you upright
His blanket of peace
Is covering you

His mercy flows
To your inward parts

His blood cleans
Your inner man

You can not clean
Inside of you
But He can

You Are Why

Do not be afraid
Do not be dismayed
Do not be ashamed
For you are why
I came

He came…
To remove our shame
To accept our blame
To light a flame

I will do through you
What only I can do
When you release your heart
To do as I will
There is nothing we can not do.

He Loves Me

He loves me when I'm good
And when I'm bad
He loves me when I'm happy
And when I'm sad

He loves me when I'm right
And when I'm wrong
He loves me when I'm weak
And when I'm strong

He loves me when I'm skinny
And when I'm fat
He loves me when I'm sweet
And when I'm a brat

He loves me when I laugh
And when I cry
He loves me when I'm bold
And when I'm shy

He loves me when I act mature
And when I'm a child
He loves me when I'm proper
And when I'm a little wild

I want Him to control me

I want Him to help me
Make the right choice

I love Him the most
I'll listen to His voice

He focuses on the good
Although He sees the bad in me

He gives me a chance

He knows what I can be

He Came to Give Us Life

Laugh when you feel like crying
Live when you feel like dying
Grin when you feel a frown
Turn the world right side up
When it is upside down

Smile when you feel like sighing
Speak truth when others are lying
Giggle when you feel like groaning
Receive joy when you feel like moaning

Tell a joke when you feel like grumbling
Smell a rose when you feel like mumbling
Reflect on good things that have happened in life
When your heart gets filled with worry,
Hopelessness or strife

Bring joy when there is sadness
Bring sanity when there is madness
Keep climbing the mountain
When you feel like giving up
When you think you can not handle it
Remember Jesus and His cup

He said, "Father, if it is possible
Let this cup pass from Me."

Yet, He willingly gave His life
So we could be free

The next time when you feel like
Always looking down
Lift your head up, look at the cross
As His blood fell to the ground

Life will not look so rough
If we could only see
What He did for each one of us
When He died on the tree

Casting all your care upon Him, for He cares for you.
                                        1 Peter 5:7

New Life Springs Forth

New life is springing forth
From the well inside of you

Draw water that is deep
Inside of your heart

When you are thirsty
When you are dry
My water washes
The tears that you cry

His Word tells us that He saves all of our tears in a bottle

How does He carry them into Heaven?

Do they evaporate into the atmosphere?

I wonder if angels carry them to the throne.

Does He save the fake tears?
Does He save the "feel sorry for me" tears?

I believe He saves the real ones
The truly repentant tears are His delight.

Imagine what the Lord can do with one truly repentant heart!

Repent, Let His water cleanse.

That out of your belly will flow rivers of Living Water…

And new life will springs forth, splashing on all.

Even in My Weakness

Even in my weakness
You are calling me
Even in my darkness
You are a light in me

Even in my stillness
You are moving me
Even in my staleness
You are refreshing me

Even in my sin
You have cleansed me
Even in my fear
You brought bravery

Even when I fail You
You have forgiven me
Even in my rebellion
You chased after me

Even in my emptiness
You have filled me
Even in my loneliness
You surrounded me

Even in my weakness

You have strengthened me
Even in my wildness
You have settled me

Even in my rebellion
You have humbled me
Even in my raging
You have quieted me

With your peace, kindness and love
You have gathered me back
Unto Yourself
And there I will stay

What if you:

Had a million dollars, but nothing to buy

A million tears, but you could not cry

A million stories, but no one to read to

A million songs, but no one to sing to

A million wishes, but no stars

A million highways, but no cars

A million fruit trees, but no fruit

A million plants, but no roots

A million children, but no one to feed them

A million followers, but no one to lead them

A million feet, but no where to walk

A million mouths, but you can not talk

A million wardrobes, but no place to wear it

A million gifts, but no one to share it

A million problems, but no solutions

A million governments, but no constitutions

The Lost Sheep

It was a beautiful sunrise. The warmth of the sun gradually nudged Wild-Olive-Root to open his eyes. Wild-Olive-Root was his full name. His Shepherd had chosen his name because He saw the new lamb's adventurous characteristics. His nickname was Rooty. As Rooty lay there, trying to awaken, he smelled the fresh air that carried the fragrance of the rose bush that was blooming near the side of the house. He raised his head and stuck his nose in the air to take in other aromas. He opened his mouth to breathe in the freshness that surrounded him. He glanced to the right and saw the grass glistening like diamonds. "Everything that my Shepherd created is beautiful!" he exclaimed. Everything is so fresh and new. A new day! A new day! A new day, to romp and play!

A new day, full of new adventures was on his mind as he ran full-speed toward the other sheep in his flock who were peacefully sleeping. "Wake up, you Sleepy Sheepies!" he cried as he flew toward them in mid-air. The other sheep woke up in surprise as they saw Rooty flying toward them. Some shielded their eyes, and others tried to duck under a bench. But they knew they could not stop what had already been started and that they were in for a "rude awakening." Some laughed and played with him. Others didn't. Some of the older sheep were very serious sheep and were often annoyed by the younger, more frisky lambs. Other older sheep teased him by saying, "Newby, Sheepie, why won't you let us sleep-ie." They added in a sing-song voice, "New-lambs, Ewe-lambs....You better not mess with the older rams!" Even some of the serious sheep snickered at the younger lambs taunts. The younger sheep ran off, kicking their feet in the air. The older, serious sheep chewed grass as they awaited for the Shepherd Who they knew would soon be arriving.

The Shepherd told them He would take them for a long walk where they could eat some tall grass in a meadow they had never been to before. There was talk that they may be going to a new river with fresh, clear water. Following the Shepherd was something they anticipated every morning. Old and young lambs alike could barely wait to see the Shepherd. The older sheep were just more reserved and proper as they waited. They knew their walk would never be boring and would always be fresh and new, just like the new day they were living in.

The leader of the sheep, who was in charge of giving instructions when the Shepherd was away, raised his voice. "Baaaa-baaa-ba-baaaa." The sheep knew they needed to stop their play and direct their attention toward Wisdom2. All the sheep, except Rooty, gathered around Wisdom2. Rooty was occupied by watching a butterfly on the other side of the yard. Wisdom2 gave his call again, and Rooty looked up to see all of the lambs looking toward him. He meandered over to the group and was quiet. He had learned to be quiet, especially after he had to be called....twice.

Wisdom2 began his instructions that he had to teach them daily. He knew that sheep can sometimes be forgetful, and that it was best to over-teach them, than to hope they would remember the rules. He began his safety rules, but Rooty was interested in a cloud formation that was drifting by the sun. Although Rooty knew the safety rules, he was one of the forgetful sheep that was mentioned earlier.

Wisdom2 had just finished his instructions when they all glanced to the right as a beam of light caught their eyes. They felt the earth shake and they knew their Shepherd was near. In the distance, they saw Him walking toward them with His staff in His hand. They ran toward Him, as they kicked their feet in the air with joy. He greeted each one with a hug and took time with them individually before they set off.

He said, "Lambs, let's go!" All of the lambs, including Rooty, loved their Shepherd and followed Him wherever He lead them. Their first stop was in the meadow He told them about. The grass was as luxurious as He had described it to be. Their hungry bellies were full as they ran. Their Shepherd teased them as they trotted and played, "Full belly, full belly, like a bowl full of jelly." They laughed and ran and played with Him for a long time. They played so long and hard, that they became thirsty.

He said, "Lambs! Let's go to the new river I told you about." As they walked toward the river, He filled their hearts with stories full of adventure with lessons entrenched in them. Soon, the river was in their sight and it was just as beautiful as He said it would be. Crystal clear water flowed downstream. It was so clear that you could see the multi-colored rocks that looked like gems when the sun beamed down on the water. Rooty said, "Wow! A rainbow in the water!" The other sheep liked how he described that river, so they asked the Shepherd if they could give the river a name that described its beauty. Rooty shouted, How about Rainbow River?!" He agreed and allowed that to be the river's name. Rooty was excited that he thought of the name for the new river, and even more excited that his Shepherd allowed it to be its name.

The river was still quite a distance away. As they were near the river's-edge, Rooty became distracted by a beautiful flowering tree in the distance. It was surrounded by a forest that caused a shadowy darkness. He was thinking, I bet those flowers are scrumptious. They reached the water's edge and he was still looking at the beautiful tree, when he heard a splash and a cry for help. Rooty's friend, Restored, had slipped and fell into the river. Restored was his best friend and he knew he would go downstream. Rooty saw the Shepherd jump in to save his friend. But instead of waiting and trusting the Shepherd to save Restored, he took off running the way the river was flowing. He allowed a doubting thought to consume him. "What if the Shepherd does not catch him, and he goes downstream?" Urged on by that thought, Rooty began running toward the beautiful tree. He saw a path through the forest that looked like a shortcut to the river. Along the path, there were more beautiful trees. "How could such beauty be dangerous?", he thought. But as he ran deeper into the forest, he noticed that the trees began to look dead, and no life seemed to be in them. He went down another path, thinking it would lead him to the Rainbow River...the river of life. But he found out that it did not lead to the river. With every step, he became more lost, alone.....and frightened.

He was hungry, and did find one tree that was like the beautiful tree he saw at the entrance of the forest. Its beautiful flowers grew on its branches, and fruit dangled from the tree. Since the fruit was within reach, he ate and rested there for a few minutes.

There he pondered what he had done. Although he had been warned repeatedly not to wander off from the flock, he had let the temptation of the beautiful flowers and thoughts of his friend's danger, overtake his sensibilities. He could not find his way back, although he tried with all of his might to remember how to get to the meadow.

Near the river's edge, Restored was laying his head on the Shepherd's lap. He was traumatized, even though it only took seconds for the Shepherd to pull him out of the river with his staff. The other sheep were so upset about Restored, they had all been resting for awhile. As Wisdom2 looked around at the resting sheep, it was then that he noticed that Rooty was not resting with them. He rushed to the Shepherd's side and told Him that Rooty was missing. The Shepherd took his shofar and blew four quick blows, and then a high pitched note. This alerted the under-shepherd that He was in need of help. The under-shepherd arrived as quickly as possible and took the 99 sheep back to the fold.

The Shepherd immediately started searching for Rooty. He yelled his name loudly, but Rooty had ventured so deeply into the woods, that He could not hear the Shepherd's voice.

The sun was setting, and Rooty thought he needed to start

walking again. In the distance, he saw two animals. At first, he was frightened, because they looked like a wolf that had been near their barn one night. But they were not large like the one he had seen. They were as small as he was and were frolicking in the grass. They were playing games like he and his friends played. He had been walking for such a long time and was very lonely and thirsty. Maybe they know a new path to the river, he thought. And besides that, they were having fun. Natural instincts of fear vanished as his need for companionship and water, overtook his caution. He ran to them and introduced himself. Startled, they stopped their play in disbelief when they realized a lamb was alone in their part of the forest. With ulterior motives, they agreed to play with him. They first showed him the way to a small puddle of water that had enough water to quench their thirst. Rooty rejoiced at finding what he thought were new friends and began playing with them. He bounded toward the wolves, and lept over them and rolled in the grass. The wolves did the same to him and they played for a long time in the meadow.

The Shepherd had sensed which way Rooty had gone. He sensed evil in the forest and could smell the wolves that he knew were there. He was close to finding Rooty, but Rooty was not even thinking about Him because he was having so much fun. Then the wolf pups stopped playing. He noticed a change in their demeanor, and he noticed that they looked toward the forest. They nodded a slight nod at each other. It was then that he heard some leaves rustling in the distance. Then he saw her. The wolf pups' mother had come to look for them. Even wolf pups knew not to venture too far from her side. She was crouched down, then suddenly stood up.

Her figure could be seen from the light of the moon   She then lifted her head toward the moon, and howled a long, chilling howl. He looked back toward his friends, and saw that they had joined their mother and were circling around him, licking their lips.

Immediately, Rooty cried out for the Shepherd. "Shepherd! I need You!" "He loudly repeated, "Shepherd, help me!" Just then, it was as if a flash of lightning struck. He saw a Light traveling quickly to come to him. His Shepherd appeared seemingly out of no where. He ran toward the wolves with His staff raised above His head. With one swipe of His staff, the wolves were hurled into the air and ran off because they knew they were no match for the Shepherd.

Rooty was shaking as the Shepherd gently picked him up and carried him over his shoulders. Along the journey home, the Shepherd spoke of His great love for him and warned him not to venture away from the Shepherd's lead. Rooty learned that the Shepherd will leave the other sheep and search for the one that is lost....every time. He listened as the Shepherd told him one story after another until they arrived home. When they got to the meadow, he saw that the other sheep were sleeping. The Shepherd gently laid Rooty beside them. Rooty looked up with tears in his eyes and said, "I'm so sorry Shepherd. I won't ever do this again. Thank You for loving me enough to come and save me, even in my rebellion." The Shepherd smiled, kissed him on the cheek, and told him to rest now. They had a new meadow to explore tomorrow. He further explained that the meadow was near the Rainbow River, just further downstream. And He added with a smile,

"This time you'll get to drink pure water from the Rainbow River, instead of muddy water out of a puddle. He smiled and said goodnight. Rooty smiled back and closed his eyes and fell asleep.

The next day, the sun again nudged Rooty into awakening. He woke up a little more serious today. Since he was the first sheep who had awakened, he thought he might be more kind when he roused the other sheep. This day...Rooty would trust the Shepherd. This day...Rooty would play. This day... Rooty would listen. This day...Rooty would obey. This day... He would follow his Shepherd wherever He leads.

Justice

The Lord our God

Is a mighty God

When justice rolls like a river

His love will save and deliver

Many will call when the nations shake

Many will call when the nations quake

Many will call

Many will fall

On their knees

In worship

He will gather them

And bestow His love upon them

Justice calls!

Justice fall!

Kelly Taylor Nutt, Copyright © 2016

Rest

Sit with Me awhile
Sit with Me awhile
Rest with Me awhile
And smile

For I will come to you
Lay all that hinders aside
My arms are open wide
So come to Me
Come to Me
And hide.....
Inside

My heart is love
Inside My heart is rest
Inside My wings of shelter
Lay your head upon
My chest

And rest

Rest....rest.....rest

Arrow in My Quiver

He is the arrow in my quiver
The jewels in my crown
A Rock in my pocket
When it is going down, down, down

He is our illumination
The Bright and Morning Star
The light in our darkness
The spark that lights our heart

When it all goes down, down, down
We will not drown, drown, drown
He will lift us up

He is our mighty weapon
Our sword and shield
Our victor in the conflict
Commander on the battle-field

His love is His weapon
The strongest weapon of all
Its power is unfathomable

Causing the enemy to fall

Love flowing down, down, down
No more prisoners bound, bound, bound
He will lift them up

Sour Pickle

Pickle, pickle, sour pickle
I am gonna tickle, tickle

Tickle until you laugh all day
We will run and dance and sing and play

Joy is coming
Joy and song
We will laugh out loud
All day long

I will tickle your heart
Until you see
How much fun life can be

Laughter and joy can be found
When you can not see fun
Anywhere around

The seemingly complex problems will not matter
Because I, the Lord, am full of laughter

You will laugh when you want to cry
Kiss that sour pickle goodbye

The Lost Child's Wilderness

Feeling abandoned and alone, the lost child sat on a rock dangling her feet in the creek. She had walked deep into the forest to a rock that was partly immersed in the water, and the other part of the rock was flat and large. This rock carried many good memories of the time when she was a child. She and her Dad had jumped into the water off of it. Swimming was her favorite activity, just as it was her Dad's. She and her Mom had fished here many times. During her teen years, she used to walk to the rock and sit and daydream. She sometimes wrote in her diary as she sat there.

Today, she was deep in thought as she remembered the things her Mom had taught her when she was young. Her Mom had passed away a week prior to her journey to this place. How she missed her! Tears stung her eyes and flowed down her cheeks and landed in the water. Memories of a mother who took care of her, stood by her and always prayed for her, filled her heart. She remembered her witty sense of humor. She remembered always having enough food and the wonderful meals she cooked for her. Being an only child, she lavished all the attention she received from her parents.

Her Dad had passed several years before and memories of him came into her mind as well. She thought of all the good times they had together. Their steadfast belief and trust in God had shaped who she was.

But this lost child began thinking of her rebellion, turning from God, her parents and everything they had taught her. As she sat there, she remembered the argument that had separated them for a season. Her parents had been pleading with her for hours. Her car was packed with all of her belongings. She had one foot outside of the car, seemingly trying to get her to stay. "If I would have just kept that foot on the ground and gotten back out of the car and joined my parents, my life would have been so different," she pondered.

She remembered looking at her parents who stood on the porch one last time. Grief was on their faces as they stood there. The last thing she heard her Mom say was, "Jesus loves you and we will always love you no matter what happens." Her foot remained on the ground as she hesitated for a moment, but then she placed her foot inside the car, slammed the door and put the car in reverse. The reverse direction of all she had been taught began as she backed out of the driveway. Her journey to the wilderness had begun.

As she thought about the time when she left her parents, tears multiplied until they turned into sobs. Thankfully she had reconciled with her parents before they died. But she had not yet been reconciled to the One they served.

She began remembering all of the things that happened during her wilderness time. She remembered the times that she really liked being alone, but also the times she hated it. She did not have any siblings, her friends had forsaken her and she did not feel like she could talk to her parents. She reasoned that they would just keep preaching at her. She poured herself into her job and would come home to an apartment full of emptiness. Being lonely overwhelmed her at times, but she would fill her time by watching television or reading a book.

Today, she felt completely alone. But she was not. Jesus had been with her from the time her foot pushed the accelerator to leave her parents until today. He had been there during every step of her journey. It was Jesus that lead her deep into the forest to this rock. This place of beauty, sitting on this rock would be the exact spot she would meet her Saviour. Her Mother's words seemed to be amplified and continuously repeated in her heart. She could almost hear her Mother's voice, "Remember, Jesus loves you, and we will always love you no matter what happens."

She remembered how she found the second part of these words to be true. Their unconditional love had welcomed her back home many years ago. But her rebellion and stubbornness had not let her return to the One her parents loved, the One who loved her.

Finally, the words of her Mother became so overpowering and loud that it drowned her rebellion. "Remember, Jesus loves you.....Jesus loves you." And there, sitting on the rock she lifted her eyes to Him and repented. Sitting in her wilderness, she asked Jesus into her heart. Jesus came into her heart in that instant. They sat on that Rock and talked for hours. She cried as He spoke. She spoke and He cried tears of joy. The sun was lowering, so she decided to go back to her home. Her home that would no longer be filled with emptiness.

Coupled with grief and lack of food, she had little strength for the journey back to her car. Jesus picked her up, put His arm around her and told her to lean on Him as He helped her

118

back. She complied by putting her full body-weight under His arm. As her journey out of the wilderness continued, she noticed the forest looked more beautiful. The flowers smelled sweeter. It seemed like even the birds sang louder and were glorifying the Lord with their song.

As they came to the clearing, the Father smiled as His Son and His new child walked toward the car. What a beautiful sight they must have been! The Father called out, "WHO IS THIS, COMING FROM THE DESERT, LEANING ON HER BELOVED!" Jesus returned a smile to the Father as He continued to lead her.

As they reached the car, He lead her to the passenger side. He assisted her in the seat and picked her foot that remained on the outside of the car and put it inside. He walked around the car and sat in the driver's seat. Then placed the keys in the ignition, and started the engine. He reached for the gears and placed the gear to......FORWARD. Thus began this once-lost child's trip out of the wilderness and to the promised land.

And Still...

I have sunk to the lowest depths
And still ....You loved me

I have stood on the highest mountain
Where Your peace surrounded me

I have sinned such deep sin
And still ....You forgave me

I have cried a river of tears
And still ....You comforted me

I have laughed until sorrow left
And You laughed with me

Your joy has filled me
Your peace has comforted me
Your loving-kindness has surrounded me
Your mercy has been extended to me
Your grace has saved me
Your blood has washed me

When I was lost, You found me
When I fell through the cracks in the road,
You picked me up
When I went down the wrong path

And Still...

You followed me
And brought me back to the place I needed to be

No one else could forgive me
Love me, be patient with me
And correct me the way You have
I have experienced life instead of death
Joy instead of sorrow
Laughter instead of tears

To You Lord, all honor, glory and praise is given

And still....I love You

How Could You Love Me?

How could You love me?
How could You forgive?
My sin was great
My sin I hate
I want again to live

Abba Father
Father and friend
Only You,
Yes, only You
Can forgive my sin
As You wash these tears
From my eyes
Could You also cleanse
What is on the inside?

He responds:

How could I not love you?
How could I not forgive?
Though your sin was great
It is not too late
I want you again to live

My child, My friend
Only you can bring to Me

Each and every sin
I will treasure every repentant tear
And what is on the inside
Bring your sins before Me
Do not run and hide…

My bride
My bride, do not hide.

The only place I desire you
to hide...
Is in the shelter of My wings

My bride
My bride, do not run.

The only place I desire you
to run...
Is into the safety of My arms.

I Missed You

Every day that went by
You were a part of my life
Every day I was gone,
I missed You
But I would come back again
And You would forgive me then
Yes, Jesus, I missed You
I missed You
Every day I was away
I missed You
But I came back again
I missed You
Every night of my life
I missed my very best Friend

Then one day in my life
I ran away from the strife
Into Your arms I found peace
All of my sorrow ceased
Although I thought I got away
I really did not
You were always there
With Your love to share
You found me when I thought I was hidden
You found me

You found me!
Although I thought I was hidden
You searched until You brought me home
Carried me through the valley
And seated me near Your throne

The Broken Glass

One day I was sitting in my room when I felt like the Lord spoke to me. He said, "Your past has been like broken glass." I kept a diary. So, I picked up my pen, opened my diary to the next blank page, and wrote down what He said. I questioned that I might have misunderstood Him, so I crossed through the words "broken glass" and wrote, "brokenness" above them. The next day, I heard a song on the radio. One of the lines in the song said, "My life has been like broken glass." So I had heard Him correctly!

I was very tired, so I closed my diary and laid my pen on top of it. I drifted off to sleep and into a dream. In the dream, I was admiring one of my favorite pieces of china that had been passed down from three generations. It was a hand-painted plate with the words, "He came to heal the broken-hearted" painted across the top of the it. A heart that had been mended was drawn in the middle and center of the china. Below the heart was Jesus' hands putting the heart back together. It was my favorite piece of my inherited dowry and I cherished it. It was more than a plate to me. It contained memories of my mother, my grandmother and my great-grandmother.

After I had held it for awhile, I reached up to put it back in its place in the china cabinet. When I did, I lost my footing and dropped the plate. It seemed to fall to the floor in slow motion, and I watched it crash and splinter into what seemed like a million pieces. I gasped in horror as all my memories of my family were broken into a pile of jagged pieces of glass scattered across the room.

As I left to get the broom and dustpan, I stepped on a small sliver of glass and it became embedded in my foot. Even though it hurt, I kept walking so I could finish the monumental task that was before me. I was determined to see my plate restored to its former beauty. I had almost gotten the pieces swept up, so I started toward the table with a large bowl that I placed there to put the broken pieces into. Near the table was a large section of glass that had been unnoticed. When I stepped near the table, I brushed my leg across it, resulting in a gaping wound that I knew I could not ignore. I went into the bathroom, so I could clean and close the wound. I placed a dressing to cover it and sat on a chair at the table.

My friend had called during this time and was aware that I had broken my plate. She came over to see if there was anything she could do. She looked at the broken pieces and didn't say anything. But I somehow knew what she was thinking. We talked for a long time, and as she turned to leave, another piece of glass that I missed wounded her leg as well. I helped her clean and bandage it as I apologized profusely. She gave me a hug and left to go home.

As I looked into the bowl I was overwhelmed with the task ahead of me. I knew that I would need the best glue, steady hands, an enormous amount of patience, and a lot of time. Days turned into weeks as I painstakingly tried to find the matching pieces. It was like a complex puzzle, and I soon realized that even if I got it back together, it would not be as beautiful as it once was.

The large gaping wound on my leg had healed by this time. But in my eagerness to get started, I had forgotten about the small sliver of glass that remained in my foot. My foot began to ache when I stepped down on it, so I looked at it and saw that it was red and swollen. It was then that I remembered about the sliver of glass. I got out my needle, and removed it. It was painful, but I knew if I did not remove it now, I would have more problems than a broken plate.

One night I was exhausted. I had tried to get the pieces back together exactly as it was before. I became impatient and decided that it would be best to give up. I cried as I began walking to put it in a cabinet in a box. I could not bring myself to throw it away.

As I opened the cabinet, I heard a knock at the door. I opened the door, and saw that it was Jesus. I was so happy to see Him, that I forgot about my broken plate. We exchanged greetings and talked for awhile. He then asked me what was in the box and I told Him what had happened. He offered to fix the plate for me. He asked me, "Would you like to see me make this plate more beautiful than it was before?" I gladly handed Him the box and we walked toward the table. We sat down and I listened as He spoke to me as He began to repair my plate.

I watched Him carefully bring the pieces together and was mesmerized at His ability to replace every sliver of glass into its rightful place. He accomplished more in one hour than I had in months. His hands were steady, as steady as His heartbeat. He was patient, and He did not need glue. His blood was the sealant and brought this vessel back to its original beauty. But He added extra touches of His glory, His grace, and His light. At last, the plate was complete. He held it up and light radiated from it in every direction. His image was sealed around the broken heart in the middle. I should have seen my image as well, as I held it in front of my face, but the only reflection in the plate was His, not mine.

With a grateful heart I clung to Him and cried. I said, "Jesus! When You touch anything, You make it beautiful! Thank You that You took the time to come by and repair something that was dear to my heart!" He replied, "Thank You for accepting my offer to repair it." I instinctively knew that there was more to what He said and that He was referring to something else along with the plate.

I asked Him to sit down and rest awhile. I took the bottle of pure water He brought with Him, and poured it into two cups. I knew He had something He wanted to share with me, so I sat quietly and drank the water He provided.. He looked at me with eyes of pure love and opened His mouth, and taught me. He began by saying, "The broken plate represents your life. Although the plate was beautiful before it was broken, along with it were generational areas of sin that were passed down and that you partook of yourself. One of My children bought and gave it to your great-grandmother before she came to know Me. She came to know me as her Savior and cherished the plate as much as you do. She desired that it be passed down to each succeeding generation as a reminder of my healing power of broken hearts.

The wounds you received were a lesson I wanted to show you as well. Throughout your life, there have been times that others have wounded you. There have been times that you have wounded others, the same as when your friend cut her foot on the piece of glass that you were unaware was still on the floor. Sometimes the large gaping wounds are easier to fix, because they are more noticeable. But sometimes they are not so easy. Sometimes the tiny slivers do the most damage because they stay hidden where you can not see them, and you forget about removing the intruder until it festers up and causes more pain. That is why you need to deal with small offenses quickly by forgiving and getting rid of it before it turns into a full-blown infection. The size of the wound is irrelevant. It is Who brings the healing that matters. That is why you need to bring everything to Me and let Me do the repairing. Because ultimately, I am the only One who can heal anything. I am the only One who can take a heart that is broken into a million pieces and put it back together again. I am the only One who can change the hearts of mankind. I have watched you look back at your life. I have seen that you are unable to forgive yourself for the trails of broken pieces of your plate along the way. Large pieces as well as slivers. And what is so awesome about Me, is that I can find all of the hidden pieces and bring them back together again. Not one sliver will I leave under a chair. I, and I alone can make your heart whole again."

Tears began flowing as I finally realized what He was trying to tell me. I cried out in repentance and joy as His truth melted and saturated my heart. No longer would I try to repair things on my own! No longer would I look at my past and the broken pieces along the way. I would see myself as He sees me, the beautiful plate that He designed. No longer will I attempt to repair something only He can repair. I am going to hand that box of broken pieces to Him and watch as He does the work. I will do what He tells me I need to do along the way, but I will no longer strive to repair something that is humanly impossible to fix on my own.

Jesus, without You, we are nothing but a pile of broken pieces of earthen vessels. But with just one touch, You can bring those broken pieces together to create a vessel. A new vessel that contains in our hearts, Your heart. A new vessel for You to work through. A new vessel that You desire to be yours. A vessel that glows with Your light and overflows and spills Your love to the rest of the broken pieces that are scattered throughout the earth.

Thank You Lord.

Set Me as a Seal Upon Your Heart

Set me as a seal upon Your heart, a seal upon Your arm...
Song of Solomon 8:6a

I lift my voice, I raise my hands
To the King of all creation
To the King of all the land

I lift my heart, I lift my soul
To the King of the nations
To the One who made me whole
I lift my voice

Oh my Beloved...

Your eyes are beautiful
Your ears hear our prayers
Your mouth speaks truth
Your hands hold our cares

Your arms are full of strength
And holds us as we cry
Lord of Lords, King of Kings
Is written on Your thigh

Your eyes are light, Your eyes are fire
Your eyes see beyond

Set Me as a Seal Upon Your Heart

Sin and wrong desire
Your ears hear us
As we cry to You
You hear a babie's cry
And all creation too

I lift my voice, O my Beloved
Your mouth speaks words of love
To Your bride
Words from above

To change us from the inside
You change our hearts
You change our mind

With words of compassion, words so kind
O My beloved, set me as a seal upon…

Your heart, Your heart, Your heart

The Battle

One day I was praying. I asked Jesus, "What is going on in Heaven today?" He replied, "We are getting ready for battle."

I saw Jesus sitting on a white stallion. He reached down and pulled me on to the horse and I sat behind Him. He took the reigns and did not give any commands to the horse. It seemed to instinctively know what to do and where we were going. It was very still and quiet along the path. The only noise I heard was a beautiful song that He sang to me as we rode along the country-side. The horse seemed to enjoy the beautiful words that flowed from the Saviour's mouth as much as I did.

It reminded me of a scene from a movie where you see an obviously in-love couple riding on a horse. It seemed like we were riding in slow motion. The beauty of the forest and the sound of the horse galloping coupled with my deep love for Him, made me want to ride and never get off the horse. Soon the horse slowed, then halted. Jesus got off the horse and assisted me to the ground.

With our swords drawn, we set out for battle. As we began walking, I was looking at the battlefield. It appeared to me that we were too late. Multitudes of people were there. Many looked like they had been mortally wounded. All that remained of many were skeletons. Still others were sitting down, weary from battle. They did not seem coherent and were oblivious to the battle that was raging around them. Some had given up and surrendered their hearts to what seemed like defeat. Others laid face-down in prayer. Some continued to pray and worship even though their wounds inhibited them from fighting until they could be healed. Others were smiling and worshiping joyfully, fully expecting His help.

I asked, "Jesus, why did we stop here? We are too late!" He didn't answer me right away, because He was busy ministering to each one. As I watched Him touch the wounded warriors, I saw an amazing thing happen. They rose up with a new determination and strength. But the one thing I noticed more than anything else, was what I saw in their eyes. Those who had been staring incoherently into space, now had eyes filled with hope, compassion and most importantly, love. Their eyes reminded me of His. One look from His eyes with love pouring out of them always brought a deeper love in my heart for Him.

As I continued to watch Him, I grew a little impatient. I heard a noise of war behind me. I heard a rattling noise, but was not sure what it was. I turned to watch another fierce battle in the distance. I thought, "We need to hurry so they won't be defeated as these warriors were." I turned back around, ready to give the Lord this suggestion. When I turned back, I was startled and jumped backwards. All who had been wounded were now clothed with heavenly armor. Even those who had been dead for a long time were now standing on their feet. Their dry bones were now full of life. Clothed in humility, they marched in unison. Clothed in His righteousness they picked up their swords and began following Him. Over each of them was a banner that read "Love."

What a dreadful sight they must have been to the enemy!

I joined the other soldiers. I reached for my sword and positioned myself behind Him as we began to walk on to the battlefield. I asked, "Jesus, what do you want me to do first?" "You need to sit over there and pray and watch." He replied. He then turned to the other warriors and repeated the same words to them. I remembered many of them from the previous battlefield. I recognized the one who sat next to me. She had been mortally wounded. She sat obediently as she worshiped Him. I objected to His instructions. I jumped up and stood before Him and said, "My weapon is ready. My sword is ready. My feet are ready. I have my armor on. My hands are ready." He listened to my argument, but gently pushed me back and said, "But child, you are not ready. Your heart is not ready. This battle is too intense for you. This battle belongs to Me." What could I say? He was right. The enemies were huge, vicious and strong. "Watch and pray. I will teach you how to fight." He instructed.

I saw Him turn and run to the battlefield. He reached for the first person. He put His arms around her. She struggled, kicked, cursed, hit Him and continued to fight for what seemed like a long time. She reminded me of a wounded animal who didn't understand that you were trying to help it. She also reminded me of a fighting fish that would not give up. It was almost as if I could hear the Lord say, "Come on guys, pray! We have caught a big one!" Again I grew impatient. I began reasoning within myself. "I think that person over there would be easier to save." The Lord looked at me and I knew I needed to focus on the one He was fighting for. I continued to watch Him until I finally saw her face begin to change. I saw her resistance lessen. The hardness of her heart began to melt. In the midst of the battle, He continued to cover her with His love. Finally, she fell to her knees in surrender.

My focus now changed to the woman who was resting and watching with me. I began to see tears over-flowing from her eyes. She then fell face-down and began sobbing. Once she composed herself and strength returned, she stood up and ran to the newly rescued woman who had fought so strongly against Jesus. Tears of joy were released as they rejoiced over the battle's end and the victory Jesus had accomplished. Jesus left them for a moment and came back to me. He knew I was questioning who these people were and how they were related.

He said, "The rebellious woman is the daughter of my warrior who had been instructed to sit next to you. Do you remember her mortal wounds? They were inflicted by her daughter. Although she continued to wound her mother, this mother never gave up on her. She cried out to Me night and day. She believed. She learned not to question Me or give Me advice. She stood on the promises I gave her from My Word. And most of all, she learned to completely trust Me and let Me fight this battle for her. Many times she would attempt to get up in the midst of the battle and try to do what only I can do. I gently put my arm in front of her and held her back and reminded her to rest and watch Me fight and win this battle for her daughter's soul. Day after day she continued to pray, believe and trust Me. She never gave up hope. What I allowed you to observe today was the end of the battle, and the victory that followed. But this battle has continued for many years. It took much patience on behalf of this mother. Her daughter continued to rebel. But My love is stronger than her sin. My love won this battle."

I watched as He then went back to this newly saved woman. He placed His banner over her. One simple word was written above her head.... "Love."

Victorious He was.

I watched as He got back on His horse and motioned me to join Him. I climbed back on the horse and we began our journey home. Suddenly, I heard the same song I heard as we were headed to the battle. His love enraptured my heart again. As we reached my destination, I turned to Him with one final question. "What is going on in Heaven tomorrow?" He just smiled and rode off.

As I watched Him I believe I heard Him reply to my heart.

"Same time. Different place. Many people. Many wounds. Many lives.
Same love. Same victory."

Fight, You Shall

You fight all day
Against the evil one
Fight you shall
But fight with the Son
Your greatest victory
Is when you
Spend time with Me
Your sweet sound
Will bring My presence down

You are Who we ask for
You are Who we seek
Crash down on us
Come down with us
Spend time with us
You are Who we seek

You war and strive all day long
Fight you shall
But fight with a song
Worship is the key
To bring victory
Worship Him
He will offer a new sound

This sound

Will shake the ground
Causing victory to arise among you

You are Who we ask for
You are Who we seek
You are Who we long for
You are our strength
When we are weak

Warrior, Ride to the Night

Warrior, warrior
Ride into the night

Warrior, warrior
Shine your light

Warrior, warrior
Help them to see

That their Saviour loves them
And will set them free

Warrior, warrior
Ride through the darkness

Warrior, warrior
Ride through the shadows

Run into the fight
And bring His light

Snatching up
And rescuing those

Caught in the thickets
Raise your sword

And cut through

The evil twines that
have wrapped themselves

Around their arms
And their legs

And are holding them
down
And preventing their escape

Cut the twines that are
suffocating
My children

Warrior, release them
Warrior, free them
And bring them to Me

142

He is Marching

Look! I see Him walking…
He is marching, marching, marching
Into battle
The lion is growling, growling after its prey

Although a whole band of shepherds
Called together against Him,
He is not afraid
So, the Lord Almighty will come down
Come down, come down (Is. 31:4)

Now, the enemy trembles and runs for cover

Sit here, He tells you. Rest, watch and learn
For this battle is not yours, it is Mine
I will fight for you.
You watch, and at times, you want to get up
And destroy the enemy
But He takes His time to come to you

He gently pushes you back
With His hand across your shoulders
You need only to trust Me and pray
That is all you need to do right now

Arrayed in holiness

He fights for His own
With expertise, He wields His sword

And with power and love,
He defeats those opposing Him
He rescues those He died for

He pierces their heart with His great love

With the precision of the Great Physician
Their heart is changed from a stony heart
Of flesh
Into a heart that seeks after His own heart
A heart that cries out as David
"Create in me a clean heart,
And renew a right spirit within me."

Victory has come
For a special chosen one
For the Lord Almighty has come down,
Come down, come down!

Even Though

Even though....

The fire may get hotter
The road may get rougher
The river may get higher
The path may get lonelier
The distractions may get louder
The mountain may get steeper

Remember....

I am above them all

Walk with Me on the rough road
Swim with Me in the raging river
Walk with Me on the path that leads to life
Climb with Me up the mountain
Walk through the fire with Me
Let your praise be louder than the distractions

And know....

That I will be with you every step of the way

The Battle Continues

I awoke this morning and asked the Lord the same question I asked yesterday. "What is going on in heaven today?" He told me we were going to the enemy's camp. As I began climbing onto the horse He asked me if I had forgotten something. I looked down at myself. I had my armor on. My bath had been taken and my hair was brushed. I saw him looking at my hands. Oh yeah, I forgot my sword and my shield. I'll be right back. After gathering my weapons I asked Him if I had forgotten anything else. He said, "No, climb up. You are ready." As I got on the horse, He turned around, looked me in the eye and said, "Do not drop your sword. I am the Word. The Word is your sword. So, I am your weapon. I am your shield. Do not forget Me. Do not march onto the battlefield until you see Me going before you." Then jokingly He added, "This is the Commander from the Wor-ship En-terprise. Today's mission- "IMPOSSIBLE."

We started the journey to the battlefield. He spoke again telling me how much He loved me. I told Him that I loved Him too. Again I heard a song. It was a new song. Filled with admiration and love, I sang it to Him as I worshiped on the back of the horse. Even though I was caught up in the moment, I came back to reality when the horse stopped. "You mean we have to get off now?" I questioned. "I want to stay here all day. I never want to leave you Jesus." He picked me up and swirled me in the air. "Neither do I want your worship to end, but I have to teach you some things." He spoke as He smiled.

In the distance I saw another battlefield. I thought I recognized a person I knew. As we grew closer, reality hit. There, with scorn on her face, was the one woman who hurt, abused, belittled and crushed me. As I looked at her, I could feel anger rising within my heart. "Jesus, please don't tell me I have to fight for her. Lord, she lied about me! She hurt my children! She stole from me!" I reminded Him of numerous incidents as they were brought to my remembrance. I finally blurted out, "Jesus, you do not understand, it is IMPOSSIBLE for me to forgive her. I do not love her. I do not even like her!"

Jesus replied, "Ok, let's get back on the horse and I will take you home if that is what you want. But do you remember the name of the mission I said we were going to complete today?" Looking down at the ground, I murmured, "Yes, Mission IMPOSSIBLE."

"I understand your pain. I also was despised and rejected of men when I was on the earth. So I understand what you went through and are going through now. With men, it is IMPOSSIBLE, but with God, all things are possible. I will be with you every step of the way. I prayed for you when I saw your heart broken into. I am the One who helped you time and time again. I caught all of your tears and I still have them. And the ones that are falling from your eyes right now, I cherish." He continued teaching me by saying, "Why do you think I told you to not let the sun go down on your wrath? And, be ye angry and sin not? It is because if you go to sleep thinking of all the things that were done TO you instead of thinking about what I have done FOR you, a root begins to grow. If it stays in your spirit too long, it will turn to bitterness and you will be defiled. But if you will listen and apply what I teach you, I can begin to grow another root inside of your heart. I can pull up that root of bitterness. I can assist you to be rooted and grounded in My love. When you keep thinking about all that she did to you, you are in chains. Those hurtful things she said have made you who you are now, because you dwell on them. And her words have been used as deadly weapons to your soul."

I could see exactly what He was talking about. The curses she had placed on me would speak the loudest when I was trying to read the word or pray. I could not focus on the Lord during these times. "Jesus!, I cried, "I need your help, I can not do this on my own. I ask you to pull this root out of me and cast it into the sea."

Forgiveness for this woman flooded me. He turned me around and I faced my enemy.

He also let me see what was happening to her spiritually. I could not believe what I saw. A hideous-looking monster surrounded her. Its claws were embedded in her and were causing much pain to her heart. Wounds covered her flesh. Many were self-inflicted. I saw her trying to escape from its clutches. The more she tried to resist, the deeper the claws went into her spirit. The longer I watched, the more I could see that she too had been despised and rejected. She could not stand who she had become. The enemy was yelling and reminding her of all she had done in the past.

Jesus turned to me and said, "Are you ready to completely forgive and pray for her now?" I was ready. I joined the Lord in the battle. It was very difficult, because the enemy was also reminding me of the things she had done to me. I said honestly, "Lord, she makes me so angry, but I ask that you release her from those who have afflicted her, including me. I have held her in as much bondage as she has held me. I pray You release both of us and Lord, release her from this beast who is wounding her. Set her free by Your power. In Your Name I pray, Amen."

Jesus said, "Amen! Now watch this." He said with authority, "satan, release this woman from bondage. Leave her alone. She is Mine. Get your claws off her. Now, GO!" I watched in amazement as that beast flew off as fast as it could. It was trying to escape from Jesus. I wondered if the same pain He inflicted on Jesus was now being placed on it. It started toward me, but Jesus had instructed me to put my shield up. So it kind of bounced off and went flying at an angle, aimed toward the sea.

Immediately I looked at the woman I had hated. She was weeping and praying. Jesus was compassionately comforting her. Just then she looked up and saw me. Running to me, she fell on my neck and cried and asked for forgiveness for all that she had done. We embraced for several minutes. I looked at her and said, "I release you and forgive you. Forgive me for my anger toward you." She returned the same words to me. Then we argued back and forth about who should forgive who. I looked over and saw Jesus laughing. He said, (Mission IMPOSSIBLE???) Mission accomplished.

He Runs

He runs through the land
With fire in His eyes
Looking at you and me
He runs through the land
With fire in His hands

Give some of that fire to me Lord Jesus!
And I will run through the land
With His fire in my eyes
Because He lit the flame
He will spread His fire
Across the land
Burn in Jesus name

Blow on the fire, blow on the fire, Wind of the Spirit, blow!

He runs through the land
With a sword in His hand
Come along with Me
Children, take up the sword
And pursue all of our enemies

I will take up the sword and stand behind
My Commander and Chief
We will overturn every stone
Pursuing the killer and the thief

Run with the Sword, run with the Lord, run!

He runs through the land
With love in His heart
Changing you and me
He runs through the land
With love in His arms
Give some of that love to me Lord Jesus!

And I will run through the land
And spread Your love
I want to be a vessel You can consume
I will give Your love to everyone
Because there is always room

Run, child, Run with a heart overflowing with My love!

The Warrior Ready

The heat and the brightness of the Son awakened the sleeping warrior.

He sat on the edge of his bed, talked to his Commander for awhile, then stood up. He waited while the Lord helped him get his armor on. Kind of like Saul when he helped put his armor on David. But completely different. His armor is light.

So the warrior waited as He got every piece of armor out. He began by putting on his breastplate of righteousness. He knew JESUS IS OUR RIGHTEOUSNESS, so he waited until this piece of armor covered his heart. He waited until those hidden things that nobody knew about were cut out. He stood as He circumcised his heart and until His blood covered him and began pumping through his veins. He waited until his heartbeat was beating in sequence with Jesus' own precious heart.

He waited while the Lord put on his belt of truth. He also knew that JESUS IS THE TRUTH, so he waited until the Lord revealed anything that was a lie. Wrong motives, beliefs, and things he believed about himself could not stay when this belt was placed around him.

He watched as the Lord picked up the helmet of salvation and placed it on his head. He knew JESUS IS OUR SALVATION, so he waited until this piece of armor covered his mind. He waited until he had the mind of Christ. He waited while Jesus helped him tear down the strongholds that were built there. He helped him learn to take every thought captive. He had learned to discern the voice of the stranger and the still small voice of His Saviour.

He then sat down and let the Lord cover his feet with the gospel of peace. He knew JESUS IS OUR PEACE, so he watched and learned how to walk in His footsteps. He learned that when He followed only His lead, he would not walk in the wrong direction. Trust and peace manifested as He simply walked where He saw Him walk. He learned to go when He said go and stop when He said stop.

Then Jesus took his hand and placed His sword in his hand. He knew that the Sword of the Spirit is the Word of God. So since JESUS IS THE WORD, He is our weapon. He is the Sword in our hand, the Rock in our slingshot, the arrow in our quiver.

Jesus then took his other hand and placed the Shield of Faith in it. He knew that JESUS IS OUR SHIELD AND OUR FAITH, so He waited as Jesus revealed areas of unbelief as well as how to protect himself against darts of fire that were sent flying toward him. He learned to defeat all those in opposition to His King and himself.

The Lord directed him to the mirror. As he looked at his reflection, he jumped back. What he saw was a fierce, strong, courageous-looking warrior, with love dripping down the sides of the armor.

That was because every piece of armor was different aspects of who Jesus was. He had put on the Lord Jesus, just as the Word says to do.

He had clothed himself with humility also, knowing that pride was the very sin that had caused the enemy to fall. He had learned lesson after hard lesson that God resists the proud and gives grace to the humble.

He had learned that he was only a vessel that He could fill and move through. Oh, Jesus loved him, but he knew that what Jesus did through him, was beyond him and his abilities.

He listened to Jesus as he shared the cry of His heart.

"WARRIOR!! Be ready! Take your place in the battle of the ages. I want souls! Rise up! Fight! Arm yourself! Do not give up! Do not shut up! Be a conqueror! I died for them. I gave My life for each one. I want them in Heaven with Me for eternity. I want them as much as I wanted you. Share Me with them!"

"WARRIOR! Love them! Love them! Love them!"

Rise Up!

Rise up mighty warriors
We are going to take the land

Rise up mighty warriors
Enter into the promised land

Rise up mighty warriors
Proclaim the good news

Show His love, His light,
His power, His might

We are not going to lose
Rise up!

Rise up worship warriors
Rise up and sing

Rise up worship warriors
And glorify our King

Rise up worship warriors
Shout His praise everywhere

In church, at home and in the streets
Let His worship fill the air

Rise up!

Kelly Taylor Nutt, Copyright © 2016

One Rock

One Rock
Is all we need
One Rock
To intercede

One Rock
Aimed at the giant's head
Just one Rock
And he will be dead

One Rock....all you need is one Rock
One Rock

All you need to stand
Place the Rock in the Master's hand
Let him bring victory to you
Just one throw and the giant is through

One Rock....all we need is one Rock
One Rock

Will bring the mountain down
One Rock
And we are on solid ground

One Rock hurled through the air
Cry to the Rock
And He will be there

One Rock....
All you need is one Rock

Ask of Me

Ask of Me
And I will give unto thee
The inheritance
Of the Father
To the Son…

And I will give you the nations
As an inheritance
The uttermost part of the earth
As your possession
Joint-heirs with Jesus
All I have is yours
When you ask of Me

Lord, we ask that You
Would give unto us
The inheritance of the Father
To the Son…

And that You give us the nations
As an inheritance
The uttermost part of the earth
As Your possessions
Joint-heirs with Jesus
All You have is ours
When we ask of You

Lord, we ask You for the nations
For the people of the earth
Nation to nation
Person to person
Lord, we ask of You

Through the Muddy Water

God will help us through muddy water
God will help us get to the other side
God will open the doors of Heaven
He will fling and open them wide

God is there
The fire is raging
God is there
In the midst of it all
God is there

God is in the midst of the waters
When they rise too high
He will part them
Or walk on them with you
God is there
He is here

The Sleeping Warrior Awakens

I lay sleeping on the ground. I thought I heard something stirring, which caused me to awaken from my slumber. Resting quietly underneath the moonlit sky and the stars sparkling above me, I thought of how beautiful everything in creation was. The Lord had created such beauty for us!

A loud sound interrupted my thoughts. I heard a trumpet blow. I jumped up and dressed quickly. I grabbed my sword and shield and stood up. I began praying for the Lord to cover me with His armor, cover me with Him, cover me with His glory.

I watched as angels were bending down and shaking others who remained asleep. "Wake up warrior!" they shouted. "It is time to arise and fight for the souls of mankind! Arise children of God! Get ready! Surely the battle is raging even as I speak to you. Array yourself with light. Array yourself with His armor. Come on child, get your shield ready! Place your sword in your hand! Place the Rock in your bag and arrows in your quiver. Worship Him and watch as He covers you with His light, His life, His song, His Word, His love!"

I watched as some turned over and went back to sleep. I saw others sit up with legs outstretched, but began thinking about how tough the battle would be. Their fears convinced them to lay back down.

Still others began thinking of all the other things they needed to get accomplished that day. Others stood as I did, and were ready for the Lord to give them instructions.

Even before He arrived, I sensed in my heart a warmth, a peace, and His glory begin to cover me. I glanced at the treeline and saw a light. I knew Jesus was near. I knew He would be walking in the midst of the camp very soon.

I glanced to the right, and saw Him walking toward us. The sound of His footsteps sounded like thunder. Louder and louder was the thundering noise. "Who could sleep through this?" I thought.

Many sleeping warriors stirred as they felt His love piercing their hearts. They stood up, repented and stood at attention. He stepped closer and closer. I began to hear weeping. I heard the cries of their hearts fill the air. I heard spontaneous worship resounding in the heavens as angels, men, women and children shouted and glorified the Master.

All of the sleeping warriors had awakened and were ready. He was now in the midst of us. He smiled as He looked deeply into our eyes. His love filled us.

The whole camp became silent in awe as we saw His beauty. I then saw Him kneel down, then suddenly stand up, raise His sword in the air, and let out a war-cry that seemed to split the heavens.

The warriors and the angels spontaneously repeated the war-cry. Jesus joined His voice with ours. He turned around, put His sword in the air again and yelled out, "Charge!" We began to run with Him, knowing that we were on our way to rescue more prisoners. We knew the war-cries had caused the darkness to flee. We knew that His cry would awaken other sleeping warriors who were getting ready to join Him at His side.

Awaken warriors, awaken!

People Partnering Together

People on the left
People on the right
Come together
And fight this fight

People on the outside
People from within
Come together
And we will win

Against the powers of darkness
That attempt to destroy
But their scheming will be
annihilated
When He fills us with His joy

And peace.....And love

People in the darkness
People in the night
Are going to join sides with
The people in the Light

And that Light is Jesus
With a perfect piercing shine
His Light so bright

The enemy runs
As the glow causes them to be blind

And the false-fire will go with them
So people see the true Light
The hidden ones
Can see the Son
The path now clear and bright

The treasures who were hidden
The treasures who are seen
Will now respond and partner together
With the King of Kings!

Over

You OVERSHADOWED us and brought life
You OVERWHELM our hearts
When we think of all You have done

You want to OVERTAKE our hearts
So You can OVERFLOW out of our spirits
Into the earthly realm

You will help me OVERCOME
You are King OVER all
You hover OVER us

Desiring us to give OVER to Him...
Every cell of our hearts

Lord! Take OVER!

Jesus, Light to the Nations

So shall you see
So shall you see
So shall you see
The road ahead
of you
So shall you see
It will be
So plain to you
The road I am leading you to

So shall you see
My glory rise upon you
So shall you see
America will remain free
So shall you see
The values I have given you
So shall you see
Into tomorrow....
I am not giving up on you

So shall you see
So shall you be
A light to the nations
As I called you to be
And some say that

The light has gone dim
But I am shining through
My people once again

I am lighting the torch
Lighting the torch
And the fire will burn
For freedom once again

I Wonder

I wonder what would happen
If all of our tears were placed
Into a common vessel
Would it become a broken vase?

Broken from anger, fear and desperation
Or could the tears be mixed together
To bring unity to our nation

I wonder what would happen
If our differences were placed
Into a common vessel
And could be erased

Gone would be all bitterness and strife
Instead strength and courage
Could be built in every life

America, don't let them break us
Although our hearts are broken into

Even though our hearts are like a broken vase
Let our mingled tears be the glue

This was written on Sept. 15, 2001, 4 days after the 9/11 attacks against our nation.

Kelly Taylor Nutt, Copyright © 2001

Zion

Pray for the people of Zion

Pray for the city on a hill

Pray for their eyes to open

Beloved Israel

Pray for the remnant of Zion

Pray for their eyes to see

Resurrection power

Released in Jerusalem

To set My people free

Pray for the captives

In bondage

Pray for liberty

My blood was spilled in Zion

To set all people free

The Love - The Over-flowing

A vessel sits alone in a dark corner of a store. It is a tall vessel and the potter had made the neck twist around in odd angles. It had taken the potter a long time to achieve the look he desired. It resembled a wine bottle. It is covered in dust and a few spider webs. It has remained there for many years. Nobody has bought it, or even picked it up. The manager was just about to throw it away but he could not bring himself to discard it. There was something intriguing about it. So he decided to dust it off and clean it up. He added a touch of new paint and diagonal designs. He decided it was worth placing in the window one more time.

He placed the vessel in the display window so everyone could see it. He overheard two women as they walked by. Their remarks weren't favorable concerning it. So, at the end of the day, he decided he would pitch it in the trash.

During the night, a man was walking in the alley and noticed the vessel in the heap of trash. It was Jesus. He grabbed the vessel and held it to His chest. "This is the one of the most beautiful vessels I have seen in a long time. And I know exactly how I will use it. Its uniqueness is perfect, and when I re-finish the vessel, it will be beautiful. He completely ignored the remarks by the two women and the store-keeper who had listened to what they thought of the vessel. He never listens to the opinions and gossip of mankind as the store-keeper had done.

172

So He took the vessel home and began His work within it.

As this vessel is, so we are to Him. We, His people, are like this vessel. Often over-looked, rejected and thrown away as if we were a piece of trash, we are crushed. He desires us to understand that He wants to pour Himself in us, as He poured Himself out for us on the cross. He waits for us to remove the lid and He, Himself, will immerse our heart, flow through our veins and arteries, and fill our vessels with Himself. He wants us to allow Him to live His life through our spirit, soul and body.

We are a vessel that He longs to fill.

So, He pulls us off the shelf and calls to us...."Open your heart! I will fill you!!" We respond to His call and He releases His liquid Love until we are full. Its cleansing is like a warmth and peace that completely wraps around us. And we become a new creation.

He then places the lid so that nothing else can get in. The liquid ferments as you learn more about the Saviour and the extremely fierce love He has for us. He teaches us to love others as the fermentation process continues.

There are times when our love for Him is so overwhelming and strong that we feel as if we will explode.

That is where He wants us to remain. Completely emptied of ourselves and filled to over-flowing with His love. Over-flowing with Him.

It is then that He stops and observes the condition of His vessels. He decides that it is now time for His liquid love to be released.

He releases the lid and the result is an explosion with such power, it flies off at the speed of light. And the liquid love comes flowing out, and everyone it touches can sense the intense love of Jesus.

He releases the lid because He can be contained no longer.

174

Shout HOSANNA!

As the people
Were welcoming you into
Jerusalem,

They shouted HOSANNA!
They were declaring
That You ARE the Messiah
The long-awaited One
The hope of Israel

So we shout today

We throw our cloaks down
In honor
Preparing the path
For Your return
We lay palm branches
Before Your entry

As we declare who You are
We turn
We turn
We turn our hearts to the King

We bow in humility
As we watch You make

Your triumphant entry
In our midst

We bow in honor and worship
the Messiah
Who we proclaim
YOU ARE!

Victory is Coming!

Victory, victory, victory is coming!
Coming into the valley

The Victorious One reaches His destination
He lifts us above the opposition
And carries us to the mountain

To bring refreshing
To our thirsty and hungry souls

The Victor is mighty
His strength can pick up
The weightiness of pressure
That rests on our shoulders
He lifts it off us, and places
Our burdens upon Himself

He rides on the wings of the wind
Victory was won in the battle of the ages

Victory is coming, is coming!
To all that will trust Him
To all who wait upon the Lord

He will renew us and give us His strength
So the journey up the mountain
Won't even be difficult

Because we have learned to let Him.....
Carry us

Victory has come!!

Freedom Makes Me Jump

I'm set free
By the power of God

Set free
To be me

I'm set free
For eternity

For the power of the Lord
Set me free

Get free
From what is holding you down

Get free
From what has you bound

Get free
Jesus has the key

And He will lead you
Where you need to be

Freedom makes me jump around
Freedom protects me from being bound
Freedom lifts me in the sky
I'm no longer bound to the ground
Because I can fly

With The Lord's Help

With the Lord's help...

The wind will not blow you down
The flood will not drown you
The fire will not burn you
The taunts of the enemy will not discourage you

The liars will not convict you
The lions will not eat you
The great fish will not swallow you
The enemy will not stop you

The demons will not frighten you
The lightning will not strike you
The sword will not cut you
The arrows will not wound you

The earthquake will not shake you
The walls will not close in on you
The bear will not devour you
Goliath will not destroy you
Jezebel will not wear you down

Although the enemy may be surrounding you on all sides, God will lift you up in the midst of them. He will rescue you. He has planned your escape.
He will hide you under the shadow of His wings.

Rejoice!
He keeps His promises!

No Gravity

I do not want gravity

I do not want the world

To pull on me

I want to soar like an eagle

Sit in heavenly places

And watch the world
From His perspective

To rise above it all

To see what He does
And how He does it

I want to watch the inside
Of a heart
As it meets the King

I often wonder if it

Lights up like it did when
Resurrection power brought Jesus back to life

I wonder if there are physical changes

I want to see what happens to people
When His Spirit is drawing them

I want to see all He wants me to see

I want to do all He wants me to do

I want to see it all! I want to partner with Him!

To Be

To see His beauty
To touch His face
To feel His presence
To live in His grace

To be more like Him
To rest in His arms
To be shielded with His protection
To be safe from harm

To walk in His footsteps
To go where He goes
To stand behind Him
As we face our foes

To be immersed in His love
To stand by His side
To be His friend
To be His bride

That is where I
Always desire.....

To be

Potter's Wheel Prayer

As I go around and around on the potter's wheel, I asked what kind of vessel I would be. I knew all I needed to do was sit there, wait and be patient as He was molding me.

I understood that I could not fix myself without His help.

Around and around I went. I then realized it sometimes takes years.

My one request was that He would fix the holes, bumps and shattered areas so that He would be the only One who could get in and never leave.

My heart's desire was that I would be a vessel of honor, fit for a King. A dwelling place. His temple.

About that time, I felt Him place me in the fire. Being purified burns and sometimes the heat is so intense that I felt as if I wanted to get off the wheel.

But I chose to stay, because I could not leave the One who loves me the way He does.

Year by year, I continue to be changed.

On the potter's wheel I will remain until He takes me to be with Him.

I Want to Know You

I want to get to know
You better

I want to get to know
You more

I want to get to know
You better

You are my best friend
My best, best friend

Because the more understanding
I receive
About your character

The deeper I get
Into Your word
It is then that I realize
I do not have a clue

And once I think
That I have got You
figured out

It is then I realize
That I know nothing

I could spend 24 hours a day
Searching
And although I will never stop seeking
And never stop desiring to learn of Your ways

I have come to the conclusion that
I will only fully understand
What You want to reveal to me
In Your timing

When we see You face to face
Only then will we fully comprehend
Who You really are

Speak Through Me

He is in the the air we breathe
He is in the songs we sing

Speak through me
Help me see

You in all things

I am not alone
For Jesus lives in me
I will shout His praise
All of my days
His love is here

Open my mouth
Open my mouth
So out of it
Will flow
Words that please
Your heart

Kelly Taylor Nutt, Copyright © 2016

190

We Have Overcome

We have overcome
We have overcome
With the power of His love
Filling us
With His love

He has overflowed
He has overflowed
Overflowed our hearts with laughter
And signs follow after
Where He leads

We have overcome
We have overcome
By the power of His blood
Washing us
With His love

Over-comers
Come over!
He cries!

Who is on My side?
He asks
Who will follow me?

We will!
We answer.

Who will give up the idols
And follow Me with their whole heart?

Who will seek what I seek?
Who will speak as I speak?

Who will be so lost in Me
That they forget the things
Of this world?

And press onward to preach
The good news of My Kingdom

Over-comers, rise up!

The Stepping Out!

You see the Lord walking on the water. You notice that He is raising His arm and motioning you to come with Him. You hear Him call your name and shout, "Come to Me and let's cross this ocean together!" He could part the water if He wanted to. But at this time in your life, He is bidding you to go on an adventure with Him.

You make the decision to join Him. You place one foot over the side of the boat. The weight of your body causes the boat to rock and shift and the waves splash on the side of the vessel. Some of the water reaches into the vessel and pours over your feet.

But it does not stop you this time. Fear has been removed. You do not even test the waters to make sure there is a firm foundation. Because you know Who your foundation is. You understand that He has the ability to transform liquids into solids.

You are reminded of previous times when you put one foot out of the boat when He invited you. You let fear overtake your mind as you looked at the water instead of Him. But you determined that the next time He bids you unto the water, you will go.

So you place your other foot onto the water and step by step,

193

you make your way to the Master. You notice that Jesus is smiling and encouraging you.

When you reach Him, He grabs you and pulls you close to His side and you dance with Him among the waves and wind.

Then the winds begin to increase in strength and you notice something in the horizon. A hurricane formed and was creeping directly toward you. Jesus whispers, "Do not be afraid. For I will hold you and will not allow the storm to blow you out of My arms."

You smile at Him, and then you both turn and face the storm. It comes and settles over you and you turn your heads upward to see the eye of the hurricane directly above you. You did not shift on the water, but began dancing once again, and went with the flow....of the Spirit.

The hurricane dissipated as Jesus commanded, "Peace, be still."

You question why He did not speak to the storm before it reached you. He proclaimed, "Because I want you to understand that storms will come, but I will always hold you firmly in place."

Beneath the ocean, you hear a loud rumble and the waves beneath your feet began to shake. "Now what Jesus?", you gasp. Jesus said, "It is an earthquake and the tsunami waves will erupt." No sooner than He finished His response, a large wave pushed you up so high, you could see villages in the

194

distance. You hold on, and with joy and exhilaration you ride the waves instead of fighting them.

Faster and faster you flow and swirl around multiple times. Laughing at every turn. Then you realize you are headed toward the village and you become concerned about those who are in harm's way. Jesus lifts His hand in the air just in time and shouts, "Thus far and no more!" Abruptly, you make a 360 degree turn and the wave is directed toward the middle of the ocean as you surf toward your boat.

You are now ready to get back in the boat and go home. This time you bid Jesus to come with you because you do not want the day to end. He picks you up and walks you across the threshold of the door that is wide open. You realize you made it through the open door this time, because He carried you through it.

He begins unwinding the sails until they are almost as high as the tsunami wave, and you glide across the ocean under the moonlit sky. Peace and stillness have rested on the water for a season. And you enjoy your needed rest. And He enjoys giving it to you.

Mountain Climbing, Mountain Moving God

Who am I?
A puppet on a string?
No words to write
No songs to sing
No thoughts to think
I am given no voice
If I dare speak
I am given no choice

If I share what I know to be true
I am made to feel it was
The wrong thing to do

One more thing added
To this mountain on my shoulders
And it is going to explode
Into a million rocks and boulders

And then I will be gone
It will be too late
But the Lord called to me
"Wait child....wait!"

I'll carry you to the top
And then you will see

196

Mountain Climbing, Mountain Moving God

A different perspective
As you observe with Me

See that mountain over there?
With one word it will flee
And with a blast of my power
It will be cast into the sea.

Thank You Lord
That You removed the rocks
One at a time

And that the mountain did not
Come crashing down
As I started to climb

You rescued me from
What was trying to destroy me
From within

And You climbed with me
Up the mountain
Time and time again

He showed me a new view
And with the Lord's approval
One day we are climbing mountains
And the next, causing their removal.

Kelly Taylor Nutt, Copyright © 2016

You Will Lead

You will lead nations
You will lead kingdoms

Because the things of this world
Have passed away from your eyes

The things of this world
Are not important to you

The Kingdom has become
Bright in your eyes.....

Therefore, I will shine forth My light into you

Therefore, I will be in the midst of you

Therefore, I will build My Kingdom through you

This is the heritage of the servants of God

The Word In, The World Out

Get the Word in
Get the "world" out

Refuse fear, oppression
Sin and doubt

Let faith rise up
Pull strongholds down

Let a smile come
When you want to frown

Release joy and thanksgiving
When you feel a dart
Knowing He is working in every situation
When your world falls apart

Actually, that is exactly what we need
Lord, destroy the "world" in us
Every wrong thought, every wrong deed

Build Your love in us
Let our world become Holy ground
And as Your disciples did
Help us turn the "world" upside down

Kelly Taylor Nutt, Copyright © 2006

Send Me God!

Here am I, send me
Send me, Lord, send me.

I will climb the highest mountain
Swim the river deep

Overflow me like a fountain
As You sing while I am asleep

I will rest in the lowest valley
When I can not see my way

And soar with eagles' wings
Until night turns into day

Lord, have Your way
Have Your way Lord
Everyday.

We Don't Know

We don't know what we're doing
But we're doing

We don't know where we're going
But we're going

We don't know
We don't know
Because the Father runs the show

Submit to Him
He will bring you through it

Time and Time Again

As a youth, full of vitality and strength
I used to love to lie down and think

I once composed a poem, the subject being
Some people missed all the clouds I was seeing

People too busy, I wondered why
To see different animals as they flew by

People too busy to enjoy the sun
Falling in the west
Its work now done

I lost that poem....

Many years and four children later
I understand why
I missed the clouds as they flew by

Yes, I missed them
But I watched my children change
Like the clouds
Their lives are rearranged

Time and Time Again

One day, I'll again have time to lie down and think
My question answered
And I, like the sun
As it falls in the west

My work as a mother will be done

Or so I thought....

Kelly Taylor Nutt, Copyright © 2011

The Sound

There is a sound ascending from the earth that is increasing in intensity.

The sound is a compilation of worship that blends into one distinct voice that touches the Master's heart.

The sound of repentant tears as they splash into the bowl of intercession.

The sound of His unified, love-sick bride crying out for more of His presence.

The sound of faith and trust stirred together until it is mixed and poured out and released into the heavenly realm.

The sound of His people who have looked to the left and to the right and have searched over all the earth and have found nothing in comparison to Jesus.

The sound of joy as worshipers sing and play their instrument for one purpose....to please the heart of their King.

The sound of dancers who are so over-flowing with their love for Him, that it flows to their feet and hands and they simply cannot contain the sound. The sound is released as they step out. Each step resounds and amplifies and resembles the sound of an army stomping into battle.

The sound of the intercessors standing between heaven and earth and pleading for mercy. The sound of His people releasing hope and encouragement to each other as they see the day approaching.

These sounds are blended and melted together and poured into the bowl of intercession. It becomes so full that it has over- flowed and begins to flow like a stream and pools up at the Father's feet.

As an offering, the sound is presented before Him and the aroma is sweet to our King.

Every nation, every tribe, every tongue has contributed to this offering.

The Lord understands that His people have set everything to the side and have set themselves apart for Him and His desires only.

He notices that their hearts are wholly His.

He understands that they love Him with all of their hearts, souls, minds and strength.

He is filled with joy when He sees there is room for no other and that they have set their faces like flint to follow after Him.

He also responds with a myriad of sounds. One day, His sound will be at such a high volume, that nobody will be able to drown out that glorious release of the sounds of heaven. His glory will descend and cover the whole earth.

What a day!

In the Thunder

I hear You in the thunder

I smell Your fragrance in the rain

I feel You in the wind

As You blow away the pain

I see You in the clouds

I hear You call my name

I sense Your cleansing in me

As You wash away my stain

The lightning flashes....Your light shines

The thunder crashes....Your power revealed

The rain falls....Your tears not wasted

The wind blows....Your strength is manifest on the earth

Blow south wind, blow

Blow north wind, blow

Blow east wind, blow

Blow west wind, blow

Swirl around us God

Blow away the dross

Remove what is holding us down

Come and dwell among us

We invite You

We love You

Come, let us serve You

Rest here.

Let Him Go, Let Him Flow

The world is quietly waiting
Sensing and anticipating
There is something they need
Someone in whom to believe

Open your mouth
And let Him go
Open your eyes
And see their need

Flow, flow
Let Him flow

The world is in need of a Saviour
The world is in need of a cure
Of their broken lives
They need the One
Who is holy and pure

Open your hands
And let Him go
Open your hearts
And let Him flow

Flow, flow
Let Him flow

The world needs Who is in us
Who we have silently tucked away
How will they hear
When we are full of fear?

Share Him with them today

All Creation Worships

All the trees of the field clap their hands

All of the stars sing unto the Lamb

All of the fish in the seas

And birds in the sky

"Holy!" is their worship cry

Why is it that one group of God's creation

Has a more difficult time entering into worship?

Why is it that mankind, the very image of God Himself,

Gets so involved with life that some have no time left

To offer thanksgiving

To go outside and clap our hands with the trees

To go cry out with the rocks

To sing with the stars

To whistle with the birds

Join the symphony that is all around us

Join the chorus of Heaven

As we adore the King of Kings and Lord of Lords....

Jesus!

The Wedding Preparation

The wedding of the ages has been in the planning stages for thousands of years. The Groom anticipates the time His bride will be with Him for eternity. The Bride has been chosen. She has readied herself as she makes the final preparations for that special day. They talk to each other for hours each morning, and sometimes into the night. When they are not talking, they are thinking about each other.

The invitations have been sent out, personally engraved by the Father. The bridal gown, shoes and the veil have been fashioned and tailored by the Groom Himself.

Their rings have been fashioned by the gifted Jeweler who makes all things beautiful. The rings that would be the symbol of their mutual love.

The flowers that would decorate the sanctuary were always in bloom and ready for the day when their aroma would fill it. Millions of rose petals that will fill the aisle the bride walks down are in their storage place. Their aroma will mix with the fragrance from the other flower arrangements that will be a sweet savor unto the Lord.

The banner that will be above each of them was laid next to the flowers. This banner had one simple word embroidered across it..."LOVE."

The song that will be sung to the bride as she makes her way down the aisle has been written by Jesus Himself. The music that will be sung during their first dance has been chosen. All who will sing already know it by heart.

The candles and the candelabras are ready. Even though there is no need for light in Heaven, they are a symbol of the Groom and bride becoming One with each other.

The home for His bride has been built by the Carpenter of heaven. It was specifically built according to her desires.

The wedding vows were written long ago by the Son. The sermon has been prepared from centuries past by the Father.

The menu for the marriage supper of the Lamb has been chosen and will be prepared by the best chefs from all of His creation.

A wedding of this magnitude has been carefully thought out and prepared by the Father. He wants His Son to have the most elaborate wedding in the history of all mankind because He loves Him so much and wants the best for Him.

He anticipates this day of celebration also, but He waits until every part of the bride is ready. Jesus longs to hear His Father say, "Son, go get Your bride." The bride longs to hear Jesus say, "Come up here."

Everything is prepared for the wedding. Everything is ready. Everything is in place in Heaven, except one thing….

The Bride.

I am Engaged!

I saw Jesus
Placing an engagement ring on my finger
And in the reflection of His Glory
All the colors that reflected from the diamond
Began shining with the light that poured from His eyes

And then, in an instant
I could understand His desire to be one
He desires His colors to shine forth in us
He desires us!

He chose us to be His bride
So I say, Yes Lord. I accept this ring.
I place it on my hand
This symbol of Your love will never be removed by me

I am running to show my friends
The diamond that You chose for me
The diamond that reflects
All of the colors You created

May the colors that shine not only illuminate my hand
But go through and overtake my heart and my soul
And that I can truly be a reflection of Your beauty
You are altogether lovely
Your love is pure and without flaw

I am Engaged!

Shine Your light through this diamond I wear
I do not deserve such a beautiful gift
I can not afford to give You such a priceless ring in return
But, I give You what I have
I give You my heart and promise to commit to You
To be Your help-meet

The King has chosen me as His own!

I am so excited
I've got to tell my friends
Guess what!?
The King has asked me to be His bride!

Roses fill my room
As He courts me
He is my heart's desire!

Kelly Tayor Nutt, Copyright © 2011

Do Not Want

I do not want religion God,
I want You
I do not want idols God,
I want You
I do not want traditions of men
I want You
I do not want a false-god,
I want You!
Yes I do!

And God replies.....

I do not want a puppet, child
I want you
I do not want a robot, child
I want you
I do not want a copy-cat
I want you
I do not want religious acts
I want you

And you, and you and you
And I want you to want Me too

I want You God!
I want You

More God
More of You!
Yes I do!

I want you child!
I want you
More child!
Of you!

I want more and more and more
And more of you!
Yes I do!

How Do You Describe Him?

Jesus, how can we describe Him?
He cannot be contained
He reaches beyond obstacles
Through colors
Across boundaries
And when He rests in your heart
He stays there

I want to put my words of love in a song
But they are too strong
To only You they belong
I want to give my words of love
To only You
And ask You into my heart
Where there is room for only two
Me and You

I went to find the words
To the mountain I climbed
But they could not be found
I looked in the valley
Without success
Although I looked all around

My love for You cannot be described
Although I have tried

It can not be done
You have made my heart feel alive
Because I know, You died and won

I went deep within my heart
As I heard Your voice speaking
I found You there

You, Jesus, are the word I was
Searching for!
Indescribable Saviour

To define all You are is impossible

I Sing to You

My songs
I sing to You
To reflect the love
That is inside of me
Love I declare to You
It is the only gift
I can give
To You

My heart, my will, my soul
All cling to You
My life is Yours
I rest in Your peace
With You

My life is Yours
All my thoughts, hopes and dreams
I give to You
I want You
To replace them with Yours
So that my heart beats
In rhythm with Yours

Kelly Taylor Nutt, Copyright © 2016

Wrapped

Wrapped inside of Mary
Was the Son of God

Wrapped in swaddling clothes
He was born

Wrapped in righteousness
He lived

Wrapped in a scarlet robe
He was ridiculed

Wrapped in sorrow
He was crucified

Wrapped in burial clothes
He was buried

Wrapped in the Father's arms
He conquered……

Clothed in glory
He was resurrected!

Clothed in majesty
He is worshiped!

Clothed with might
He is honored!

Clothed in power
He reigns!!!

I Want

I want to wrestle with the strength that is in....
Your arm

I want to be an extension of....
Your hand

I want to see all that You see with....
Your eyes

I want to hear the things you hear with....
Your ears

I want to speak the words that You speak with....
Your mouth

I want to feel what You are feeling with....
Your touch

I want to think everything you think with....
Your mind

I want to feel your heart beating
Until my rhythm matches Yours

I want....

Your heart, Your heart, Your heart!

I want all of You Jesus

The Wedding Dress

One morning as I woke up, thoughts of my upcoming wedding flooded my mind. My wedding dress was neatly hung in my closet. It was covered with plastic to protect it.

I thought, "I am going to do something crazy today. I am going to put my dress, veil, and shoes on and take a walk to town." I wanted to know how it felt to walk in a dress that expressed my love for my Bridegroom. As I walked along, I pretended to be walking down the aisle, looking to the One I would be spending the rest of my life with. How I longed for my Groom to come and capture me away! I would soon be His forever!

As I walked along, I was not paying attention where I stepped. I felt a pull near the hem. I looked down to see what happened. In horror I saw a large rip around the lace. I had become entangled in thorns. As I reached down to try to remove them, I lost my balance, fell, and landed in the dirt. I became so upset that I thought about giving up and walking home. But I thought, "No, I am not going to let what happened ruin my day."

Again I walked. Further down the road, I heard a car. My eyes focused on a puddle of water. I cried out, "OH NO!" Just as I spoke those words, I heard and felt the splash. Mud now covered my dress, my veil, my shoes and the pearls I had so painstakingly sewed on it. I turned and walked back home.

When I looked in the mirror, I could not believe how dirty I had become. I cried in shame, blaming myself for being so stupid. "Why did I do that? Why did I not leave the dress covered?!" My wedding dress for our special day was now stained, wrinkled and torn!

At that moment, I heard the voice of my Groom speaking softly to my broken heart. His voice reminded me of His great love for me. He reminded me that He loves me just the way I am. He continued by saying, " I chose you. I love you. I died for you." He wiped my eyes and saved the tears.

The dress now had my tears mixed with the mud.

He continued, "Daughter, I can mend that tear in the lace. I can mend the parts of your heart that have been torn. My blood can wash all of the dirt and mud away. Remember, I am the Pearl of Great Price. After I am finished cleaning your dress, the pearls that you sewed on will be as they were before. The Wind of My Spirit will blow every wrinkle away.

So, I handed Him the dress, fully trusting Him to make it as beautiful as it was before. I laid down in peace and went to sleep.

When I woke up the next morning, I saw the dress hung on the outside of my closet. There was no protective covering on it to keep it clean.

He again spoke to me. He said, "There is no need for plastic to protect your dress, because I am your protective covering. I will keep it spotless for you, if you come to me when it needs repair." Do you want to try it on now?," He asked.

After I was completely dressed, He reminded me to always be ready.

When I looked in the mirror, I could not believe what I saw. It was so white! Whiter than anything I had seen on earth before! The hem had been mended. Not only were the pearls shining brilliantly, He had applied a diamond next to every pearl. The whole dress was covered with diamonds and pearls. And when the Light of the Son hit it, every color on earth and colors I have never seen before radiated from the dress.

As I placed the veil on my head, I felt His glory fall on the veil and then completely cover me. I bowed down because the weight of His Glory was so strong, I could no longer stand. I looked in the mirror and I saw His reflection, not mine. He was smiling with approval.

As I stood up, I heard a trumpet blow. I heard a shout, "COME UP HERE!" Before I had time to think about what was happening, I was with Him.

The Bridegroom had come!! My home He built for me was prepared.. The veil was lifted and I could see for the first time, my King, my Redeemer, my Best Friend, my Deliverer, my Husband!

I began walking down the aisle with my arm in my Father's. And forever will I share my life with the One I have waited all my life to see. Jesus!!!!!!!!!

Kelly Taylor Nutt, Copyright © 2009

The Color

You are the color in life

Rain when it is dry

You are our laughter

When tears fill our eye

You are our light

When darkness surrounds

You are the place

Where love is found

You are our warmth

When it is cold

You are our youth

When we grow old

You are our smile

When we cry

You are our life

When we die

Your colors brighten everything! Sometimes when you look out of the window everything seems dull, dreary, and monotonous. Close your eyes and ask Him to let you see Him in a new way.

Our shining Jesus paints the colors brighter.

Our loving Jesus makes burdens lighter.

Our victorious Jesus will not be defeated.

Our sharing Jesus will supply all that is needed.

Let Jesus add some color to your life! He will create a masterpiece within you. Sit still and let Him re-create you. "Me? Beautiful?" You ask. Yes, because Jesus dwells in your heart now. He is the only reason any true beauty can emerge. If you let Him, He will mix the paint and the Artist of Heaven will blend the colors in such a way, that He will cause you to shine. Only our Creator can accomplish that.

Let Him color you.

You are Amazing

You are amazing!

You are glorious!

Perfect One

Risen Son

King of Kings!

You are amazing!

You are victorious!

Spotless Lamb

Provided Ram

King of all Kings!

Sparkly-Shiny People

Who are these
Sparkly
Shiny
Beautiful-feeted
People?

They are the Lord's
Children
You can see them coming
Because....

He who sparkles
He who shines
He who makes our feet
Beautiful

Now lives within
Our hearts

Captured...

He captured my heart

He enraptured my heart

He healed every broken part

Whatever Your Call

See as a warrior sees
Decree as a watchman decrees

Sing as a singer sings
Dream as a dreamer dreams

Write as a writer writes
Fight as a soldier fights

Whatever your call....
Give your all

Preach as a preacher preaches
Teach as a teacher teaches

Prophesy as a prophet who hears
Heal the wounded, dry up the tears

Equip as an apostle builds
Sharpen your swords;
Shine your shields

Intercede as an intercessor intercedes

Feel their pain
Meet their needs

Hear the call

Give your all!

Everlasting Breath

When my journey in this life is over
and I take my last breath on this earth

I will continue to breathe
In a place where there is not such a thing
as a "last breath"

A breathing exchange will take place
As You fill my lungs with
Everlasting life

A place where we will be immersed
in a never-ending flow
of Your love

A place where Your love saturates
everything it touches

Where our heartbeat will merge
with the heartbeat of the Father

Where there are no tears
And no more pain
No more grief

And no more shame

Where His love like a river flows
And saturates our hearts and souls

A place where the healing flows
And the music starts
A place where Your love fills
And floods our hearts

There will be life instead of death
When we receive...

Your everlasting breath.

Holy

Holy, holy
Holy Lord God Almighty
Is the Lamb

He was slain
The Lamb was slain
Only He is able
To take and open the scroll
The root of David
The Bright and Morning Star

He is worthy, worthy
Worthy only is the Lamb

You are worthy O Lord to receive
Glory and honor and power
For You created all things
And for Your pleasure
They are created

We give honor, honor
Honor to the Lamb

One day those who put their trust

In Jesus
Will be in the multitude
That will shout in spontaneous praise
As we stand before the Lamb

And cry
Worthy You are
Righteous You are
Holy You are
Priceless....

You are!

The Celebration

I watched as the soldiers ahead of me took their place in line. Some turned to the left. The others turned to the right and formed two lines. Facing each other, I saw them place their hands on their swords.

I was anticipating taking my place in the line, because I knew who this celebration was for. How I longed to see my King! It was now my turn to take my place. As I looked into the eyes of the soldier directly across from me, I saw the anticipation on his face as well. I watched all the others behind me as they took their place in line.

With a command, our swords were drawn and lifted in the air. Touching the tips of the swords to the person directly across from us, we waited.

I heard many gasp as they saw the King walking toward us. We could already feel His glory before He arrived to walk under the tunnel of swords. His love was now covering us. His peace was clothing us. Step by step, He drew closer.

He was so beautiful! I could not take my eyes off the One I had waited for all of my life. His light is shining so brightly! The Mighty One was Clothed in a robe and wearing the

242

crown He should have received instead of the crown they gave Him when He died for us.

He was smiling and joy emanated from His glowing countenance. The ground seemed like it was shaking as He approached. Power was exemplified with each step. We could barely contain themselves. But we stood in silence and awe.

As He reached the first soldier under the upraised swords, I watched as He embraced each son, each daughter. Now it was my turn to be held in His arms. I looked into His eyes of purity. I cried when He said, Well done, My faithful servant, enter now into the joy of the Lord. *Matt. 25:23. NIV.*

He continued through the line until He had greeted each one. He then turned and faced us. Spontaneous praise filled the air. The Victorious One! Master! King! Saviour! The worship continued for years. Because time didn't matter anymore.

Kelly Taylor Nutt, Copyright © 2011

We Follow the Lamb

We follow the Lamb
We follow the Lamb
Where He goes we will go
What He says we will do
Forever follow the Lamb

Come and follow the Lamb
Come and follow the Lamb
By His stripes we are healed
Our salvation was sealed
The day we killed the Lamb

Do you know the Lamb
Do you know the Lamb
Our protection and shield
God's plan was revealed
The day He raised the Lamb

Bethlehem + Jerusalem = Life

I was thinking about the city God chose to use to bring everlasting life to all nations.

Bethlehem was the city He chose to bring His Son into the earthly realm.

I used to think of Jerusalem as the city where He died.

Jerusalem was the city where He was obedient unto death.

But Jerusalem was also very close to the place where He was resurrected.

In Bethlehem and Jerusalem, life came forth!

Kelly Taylor Nutt, Copyright © 2010

He's Calling Out

Lovely is He
Beautiful is He
Waiting in the midst
Of the throne
For you and me

Lovely is He
Beautiful is He
Waiting in the midst of the throne

Righteous is He
Holy is He
Waiting, waiting, waiting
For His people to turn

He is drawing all
He is drawing all
To His throne

He is calling out
He is calling out
He is calling out
From the midst of the throne

He is calling
Awaken

Awaken today
Awaken My people
Come away

In the nations
My desire is to do
What I did and so much more

I am waiting for you
I am watching for you
I am waiting on you
You think that You are waiting on Me

But I am waiting on you

The Wedding

One day Jesus finished the very last dwelling place for the last person who had accepted His marriage proposal. Word spread quickly that the bride was now complete. She was without spot or wrinkle. She had lost her desire for everything the world had offered, and had given herself wholly to Him. The Holy Spirit cried out, "Come quickly Lord Jesus!" The bride had joined Him with the same cry. All of the hosts of heaven could hear their pleas. Soon afterward Jesus heard His Father say the words he had longed to hear. With tears in His eyes, the Father said, "Son, it is time to go and get your bride." The angels were immediately sent to gather the harvest. The bride was waiting on earth and listening for the trumpet blast and His voice. Jesus opened His mouth with a shout. The trumpet was blown so loudly that all of creation heard it. In an instant, in the twinkling of an eye, the bride was joined to her Groom.

This day was like no other. It was the culmination of the reason Jesus had left Heaven and gave His life for His bride. It was the end of the life the bride once knew. It was the beginning of her life in a place that has no beginning or ending. The bride had been sealed with His blood and the seal was on her forehead. She now entered the joy of the Lord. They relished this day. The day they got to meet face to face. At no time in history was there such a glorious reunion. They took their time because they were now free from the boundaries of 24- hour periods called a day.

Soon the bride began preparing for the wedding. Carefully she was dressed in her wedding gown with assistance from the angels. Her shoes were placed on her feet. She had the engagement ring Jesus had given to her on her finger. She did not need make-up because her face glowed with the reflection of His glory. The angels helped her place the veil on her head. She pulled it over her face as a covering and waited. The angels stood in awe at such beauty that flowed out of her heart. The beauty that reflected the Son. They remembered what she looked like before she met Jesus. Such a transformation in her countenance could have only been completed by a Master Potter.

The bride waited until she heard music fill the air. She knew it was time to become one with her Groom. She began her walk down the hall that lead to the sanctuary. With each step, a different memory of what her Groom had done for her flooded her heart. She could barely contain the joy within her spirit. Each step brought her closer and closer to her Saviour. She was now near the entry of the inner sanctuary.

The Father was waiting for her there. He smiled as He took her hand and placed it in the crook of His arm. The music heightened in volume. The sounds could be heard throughout the entire universe.

The door attendants opened the closed doors. She and the Father stood at the entrance of the sanctuary. All in attendance stood in honor of the Father and to see the Son's bride.

She took a deep breath and waited for the Father to begin walking her down the aisle.

Awe filled them as their eyes were fixed on her. But her eyes were fixed on Jesus, who was waiting for her. His eyes were fixed on hers as well. His purple robe was glorious. His train filled the temple. His jeweled crown reflected all of the colors of Heaven. His countenance shone brightly. He was altogether lovely.

The music crescendoed and He began to sing to her the way He used to sing over her while she lived on the earth. He sang a song of hope. A song of deliverance. A song expressing His deep and everlasting love He felt for her.

Silently she walked with the Father. As they walked together, the rose petals that were placed along the aisle, scattered into the air, as if a Wind was blowing them. Their fragrance filled the temple. His presence and glory filled the air as they grew closer. She was glad she had the Father to help her stand because His glory was so weighty it was difficult to walk as she drew closer to Him.

She now stood beside Him. She handed the bouquet of roses and lilly of the valley flowers to the Father. He kissed her on the cheek and took her hand from His arm and placed it in the Son's hand.

The Father now took His place for all who were assembled and began by saying, "If anyone has any reason why these two should not be joined in marriage, speak now or forever hold your peace." I heard an angel snicker, then another. Soon nobody could contain their laughter as joy permeated the walls. The Father, the Son, the Holy Spirit, the bride and all of the hosts of heaven laughed as they thought of only one who would even dare to speak up at such a time as this. He tried to bring accusations against the bride for years and was now in a lake somewhere.

After the laughter subsided, the focus returned to the wedding. The Father spoke again. He began speaking to the bride. He reminded her of all that His Son had done to acquire her. He told the bride about events she did not know about and had never heard before. Each word He spoke was eloquent and it helped her understand exactly what Jesus went through and how weighty was the cost of His sacrifice. He ended by saying , "So, bride of Christ, you are the reason He died. You are one of the reasons we are here for this celebration today. You are a gift to my Son." He focused on the Son and said. "I do not even have to tell You to take care of her, because I know You always will. I give this multitude to You. She is Your help-meet. She has overcome and loves You with all that is within her. Now, enjoy each other, you have plenty of time."

We kneeled down as He prayed a blessing over the marriage. Then He had us turn toward the audience. His voice thundered as He spoke saying, "The Bride and the Groom are now ONE." The angels began worshiping loudly. The sound rang into the heavenlies as everyone joined in praise.

The angels who had protected His bride congratulated each

one. One angel teasingly congratulated the bride on the choice she made for a husband. Adding, "The best man always wins." Laughter again filled the air as we started toward the area where we would share our first dance. A new song began to play. Jesus took the bride by the hand and placed her in His arms as He lead her around the dance floor. It was a glorious moment which lasted a long time.

Then one of the angels spoke. "Is anyone hungry? It is now time for everyone to join in the marriage supper of the Lamb. The table is set. Come and eat. Come and dine on its fruits. May it always satisfy you. One by one we were lead to our seat at the table. One by one, the bride entered into His rest. We waited for our King to arrive.

Soon, the door swung open and the King majestically entered the banquet hall. Before He took His seat at the head of the table, we saw Him pause for a moment. We noticed that He seemed to be deep in thought. Then He turned around and slowly shut the door.

Enjoy these other great books from
Bold Truth Publishing

Seemed Good to
THE HOLY GHOST
by Daryl P Holloman

EFFECTIVE PRISON Ministries
by Wayne W. Sanders

Obedience is Not an Option
by Brian Ohse

KINGDOM of LIGHT 1 - kingdom of darkness
Truth about Spiritual Warfare
by Michael R. Hicks

The Holy Spirit SPEAKS Expressly
by Elizabeth Pruitt Sloan

Matthew 4:4
Man shall not live by bread alone,
but by every word that proceedeth out of the mouth of God.
by Rick McKnight

THE BLOOD COVENANT
by Ronnie Moore

C.H.P. - Coffee Has Priority
The Memoirs of a California Highway Patrol Officer - Badge 9045
by Ed Marr

PITIFUL or POWERFUL?
THE CHOICE IS YOURS
by Rachel V. Jeffries

Available at Select Bookstores and at
www.BoldTruthPublishing.com